David R. Gastfriend, MD
Editor

Addiction Treatment Matching: Research Foundations of the American Society of Addiction Medicine (ASAM) Criteri~

Addiction Treatment Matchi~ 〜 *of the*
American Society of ~iteria
has been co-published ~ictive
Diseases, Volume 22, 〜 〜〜.

Pre-publication
REVIEWS,
COMMENTARIES,
EVALUATIONS . . .

" A SINGLE-SOURCE KNOWLEDGE BANK of current research on the feasibility, utility, and need for wide utilization of PPC. . . . Chronicles the development and refinement of the PPC. . . . Demonstrates the achievement of this quantitative tool in over a decade of consensus generation, pilot testing, methods de-

. ~lopment, psychometric study, and controlled research. Gastfriend and colleagues present the definitive research and background rationale for wide adoption of the ASAM criteria, currently recommended by 20 states and implemented in 171 Veterans Administration Medical Centers and Department of Defense facilities worldwide."

Luc R. Pelletier, MSN, RN, BC, CPHQ
Editor-in-Chief
Journal for Healthcare Quality;
Project Director
Danya International, Inc.

More pre-publication
REVIEWS, COMMENTARIES, EVALUATIONS . . .

"**P**RESENTS THE SCIENCE TO SUPPORT THE USE OF THE ASAM CRITERIA, and the continuing research to increase their value for frontline clinicians treating complex patient populations. Especially useful to the future of substance abuse treatment are the initial studies of a computerized algorithm for making placement decisions and the articulation of program competencies for placing and treating persons with co-occurring mental health and addictive disorders."

Frank McCorry, PhD
Chair
Washington Circle on Performance
Measurement for Care of Substance
Use Disorders

"**A** CAREFULLY PREPARED REVIEW of the status of the patient placement criteria (PPC). . . . A SOLID CONTRIBUTION TO OUR UNDERSTANDING of matching an individual's needs to appropriate treatment resources. The book goes into detail about the current feasibility, standardization, and validation of the PPC and is a status report on both the application of the criteria and of the needs for further refinement."

David C. Lewis, MD
Professor
Medicine and Community Health
Donald G. Millar
Distinguished Professor
Alcohol and Addiction Studies
Brown University

The Haworth Medical Press
An Imprint of The Haworth Press, Inc.

Addiction Treatment Matching: Research Foundations of the American Society of Addiction Medicine (ASAM) Criteria

Addiction Treatment Matching: Research Foundations of the American Society of Addiction Medicine (ASAM) Criteria has been co-published simultaneously as *Journal of Addictive Diseases*, Volume 22, Supplement Number 1 2003.

The *Journal of Addictive Diseases* Monographic "Separates"
(formerly *Advances in Alcohol & Substance Abuse* series)*

Below is a list of "separates," which in serials librarianship means a special issue simultaneously published as a special journal issue or double-issue *and* as a "separate" hardbound monograph. (This is a format which we also call a "DocuSerial.")

"Separates" are published because specialized libraries or professionals may wish to purchase a specific thematic issue by itself in a format which can be separately cataloged and shelved, as opposed to purchasing the journal on an on-going basis. Faculty members may also more easily consider a "separate" for classroom adoption.

"Separates" are carefully classified separately with the major book jobbers so that the journal tie-in can be noted on new book order slips to avoid duplicate purchasing.

You may wish to visit Haworth's website at . . .

http://www.HaworthPress.com

. . . to search our online catalog for complete tables of contents of these separates and related publications.

You may also call 1-800-HAWORTH (outside US/Canada: 607-722-5857), or Fax 1-800-895-0582 (outside US/Canada: 607-771-0012), or e-mail at:

docdelivery@haworthpress.com

Addiction Treatment Matching: Research Foundations of the American Society of Addiction Medicine (ASAM) Criteria, edited by David R. Gastfriend, MD (Vol. 22 Suppl. 1, 2003). *Focuses on the ins and outs of the ASAM Criteria–the state-of-the-art in addictions placement matching.*

Effects of Substance Abuse Treatment on AIDS Risk Behaviors, edited by Edward Gottheil, MD, PhD (Vol. 17, No. 4, 1998). *In this important book, you will discover drug abuse treatment methods that will reduce the number of injection episodes and reduce injection use in higher risk settings, such as shooting galleries, thereby reducing your clients risk of infection.*

Smoking and Illicit Drug Use, edited by Mark S. Gold, MD (Vol. 17, No. 1, 1998). *"Based on an understanding of the brain biology of reward, Gold and his colleagues provide policymakers, clinicians, and the public with the best-ever look at the reason why 90% of the nation's more than 60 million cigarette smokers want to quit but have trouble achieving that life-saving goal." (Robert L. DuPont, MD, President, Institute for Behavior and Health, and Professor of Psychiatry, Georgetown University School of Medicine, Rockville, MD). Focuses on the addictive properties of the numerous constituents of tobacco smoke and nicotine dependency.*

The Integration of Pharmacological and Nonpharmacological Treatments in Drug/Alcohol Addictions, edited by Norman S. Miller, MD, and Barry Stimmel, MD (Vol. 16, No. 4, 1997). *Summarizes and provides the groundwork for future considerations in developing and integrating medications with the standard of care for addictions treatment.*

Intensive Outpatient Treatment for the Addictions, edited by Edward Gottheil, MD, PhD (Vol. 16, No. 2, 1997). *"An invaluable source of up-to-date information on important issues relating to IOP, including the active ingredients of successful IOP, the effectiveness of IOP, causes of early dropout, and the impact of psychiatric status and motivation for change on outcomes for patients." (Stephen Magura, PhD, Director, Institute for Treatment Research, National Development & Research institutes, Inc., New York)*

The Neurobiology of Cocaine Addiction: From Bench to Bedside, edited by Herman Joseph, PhD, and Barry Stimmel, MD (Vol. 15, No. 4, 1997). *"Provides an excellent overview of advances in the treatment of cocaine addiction." (The Annals of Pharmacotherapy)*

The Effectiveness of Social Interventions for Homeless Substance Abusers, edited by Gerald J. Stahler, PhD, and Barry Stimmel, MD (Vol. 14, No. 4, 1996). *"Any policymaker or administrator seeking to have a positive impact on the complex problems of this population would be well-advised to thoroughly digest the contents of this volume." (Journal of Behavioral Health Services & Research (formerly the Journal of Mental Health Administration))*

Experimental Therapeutics in Addiction Medicine, edited by Stephen Magura, PhD, and Andrew Rosenblum, PhD (Vol. 13, No. 3/4, 1995). *"Recommended for any clinician involved in caring for patients with substance abuse problems and for those interested in furthering research in this discipline." (The Annals of Pharmacotherapy)*

Comorbidity of Addictive and Psychiatric Disorders, edited by Norman S. Miller, MD (Vol. 12, No. 3, 1993). *"A wealth of factual information . . . it should be included in the library of every psychiatric hospital because it is an excellent reference book." (Israel Journal of Psychiatry)*

Cocaine: Physiological and Physiopathological Effects, edited by Alfonso Paredes, MD, and David A. Gorlick, MD, PhD (Vol. 11, No. 4, 1993). *"The broad range of psychiatric and medical consequences of the epidemic of cocaine use described in this volume should jolt everyone toward increasing strategies to educate, motivate, and stimulate health practitioners at all levels." (Perspectives on Addictions Nursing)*

What Works in Drug Abuse Epidemiology, edited by Blanche Frank, PhD, and Ronald Simeone, PhD (Vol. 11, No. 1, 1992). *"An excellent reference text not only for researchers and scholars, but also for administrators, policymakers, law enforcements agents, and health educators who value the importance of research in decisionmaking at both the micro and macro levels of the ever-growing substance abuse speciality." (International Journal of Epidemiology)*

Cocaine, AIDS, and Intravenous Drug Use, edited by Samuel R. Friedman, PhD, and Douglas S. Lipton, PhD (Vol. 10, No. 4, 1991). *"Examines what has been successful in treatment and prevention and raises issues to promote greater research in the fields for improved treatment and prevention of drug abuse and HIV-infection." (Sci-Tech Book News)*

Behavioral and Biochemical Issues in Substance Abuse, edited by Frank R. George, PhD, and Doris Clouet, PhD* (Vol. 10, No. 1/2, 1991). *"An excellent overview of the power of genetic experimental designs, the results that can be generated as well as the cautions that must be observed in this approach." (Contemporary Psychology)*

Addiction Potential of Abused Drugs and Drug Classes, edited by Carlton K. Erikson, PhD, Martin A. Javors, PhD, and William W. Morgan, PhD* (Vol. 9, No. 1/2, 1990). *"A good reference book for anyone who works in the drug abuse field, particularly those who have responsibilities in the area of community education." (Journal of Psychoactive Drugs)*

Alcohol Research from Bench to Bedside, edited by Enoch Gordis, MD, Boris Tabakoff, PhD, and Markku Linnoila, MD, PhD* (Vol. 7, No. 3/4, 1989). *Scientists and clinicians examine the exciting endeavors in science that have produced medical knowledge applicable to a wide spectrum of treatment and prevention efforts.*

AIDS and Substance Abuse, edited by Larry Siegel, MD* (Vol. 7, No. 2, 1988). *"Contributes in a worthwhile fashion to a number of debates." (British Journal of Addiction)*

Pharmacological Issues in Alcohol and Substance Abuse, edited by Barry Stimmel, MD* (Vol. 7, No. 1, 1988). *"Good reference book for the knowledge of the pharmacology of certain drugs used in treating chemically dependent cases." (Anthony B. Radcliffe, MD, Physician in Charge, Chemical Recovery Program, Kaiser, Pontana, California)*

Children of Alcoholics, edited by Margaret Bean-Bayog, MD, and Barry Stimmel, MD* (Vol. 6, No. 4, 1988). *"This comprehensive volume examines significant research and clinical development in this area." (T.H.E. Journal)*

Cocaine: Pharmacology, Addiction, and Therapy, edited by Mark S. Gold, MD, Marc Galanter, MD, and Barry Stimmel, MD* (Vol. 6, No. 2, 1987). *"Diagnosis and treatment methods are also explored in this highly useful and informative book." (Journal of the American Association of Psychiatric Administrators)*

Alcohol and Substance Abuse in Women and Children, edited by Barry Stimmel, MD* (Vol. 5, No. 3, 1986). *Here is a timely volume that examines the problems of substance abuse in women and children, with a particular emphasis on the role played by the family in the development and perpetuation of the problem.*

Controversies in Alcoholism and Substance Abuse, edited by Barry Stimmel, MD* (Vol. 5, No. 1/2, 1986). *"Thorough, well-informed, and up-to-date." (The British Journal of Psychiatry)*

Alcohol and Substance Abuse in Adolescence, edited by Judith S. Brook, EdD, Dan Lettieri, PhD, David W. Brook, MD, and Barry Stimmel, MD* (Vol. 4, No. 3/4, 1985). *"Contains considerable information that would be useful to mental health clinicians and primary care physicians who deal extensively with adolescents." (The New England Journal of Medicine)*

Alcohol and Drug Abuse in the Affluent, edited by Barry Stimmel, MD* (Vol. 4, No. 2, 1984). *"A valuable contribution to drug abuse literature presenting data on a hitherto under-researched population of drug users." (British Journal of Addiction)*

Cultural and Sociological Aspects of Alcoholism and Substance Abuse, edited by Barry Stimmel, MD* (Vol. 4, No. 1, 1984). *Experts explore the relationship of such factors as ethnicity, family, religion, and gender to chemical abuse and address important implications for treatment.*

Dual Addiction: Pharmacological Issues in the Treatment of Concomitant Alcoholism and Drug Abuse, edited by Mary Jeanne Kreek, MD, and Barry Stimmel, MD* (Vol. 3, No. 4, 1984). *"Provides a good overview of dual addiction." (Contemporary Psychology)*

Conceptual Issues in Alcoholism and Substance Abuse, edited by Joyce H. Lowinson, MD, and Barry Stimmel, MD* (Vol. 3, No. 3, 1984). *This timely volume emphasizes the relevance of current, basic research to the clinical management of the substance abuser.*

The Addictive Behaviors, edited by Howard Shaffer, PhD, and Barry Stimmel, MD* (Vol. 3, No. 1/2, 1984). *"Remarkable . . . is the book's capacity to illustrate social myths and models, to challenge them, and to direct substance abuse professionals in their clinical and research inquiries." (Journal of Psychoactive Drugs)*

Psychosocial Constructs of Alcoholism and Substance Abuse, edited by Barry Stimmel, MD* (Vol. 2, No. 4, 1983). *"An excellent vehicle for orienting interested readers toward critical reference materials and important psychosocial issues." (Bulletin of the Society of Psychologists in Addictive Behaviors)*

Federal Priorities in Funding Alcohol and Drug Abuse Programs, edited by Barry Stimmel, MD* (Vol. 2, No. 3, 1983). *Reveals and evaluates current federal funding for chemical abuse treatment problems.*

Current Controversies in Alcoholism, edited by Barry Stimmel, MD* (Vol. 2, No. 2, 1983). *"Articles vary from reports of sophisticated research to essays backed by thorough literature reviews." (Choice)*

Evaluation of Drug Treatment Programs, edited by Barry Stimmel, MD* (Vol. 2, No. 1, 1983). *"Provides the reader with a unique perspective on the effectiveness of drug treatment programs." (American Journal of Pharmaceutical Education)*

Effects of Maternal Alcohol and Drug Abuse on the Newborn, edited by Barry Stimmel, MD* (Vol. 1, No. 3/4, 1982). *"Authoritative and thought-provoking . . . should be carefully studied by those responsible for the management of drug addiction, and especially by obstetricians and neonatal pediatricians." (The British Journal of Psychiatry)*

Recent Advances in the Biology of Alcoholism, edited by Charles S. Lieber, MD, and Barry Stimmel, MD* (Vol. 1, No. 2, 1982). *"A very valuable handbook for researchers and clinicians interested in alcohol metabolism and its interaction with other drugs, and the endocrine system." (Journal of Studies on Alcohol)*

Opiate Receptors, Neurotransmitters, and Drug Dependence: Basic Science-Clinical Correlates, edited by Barry Stimmel, MD* (Vol. 1, No. 1, 1981). *"An exciting, extensive, and innovative approach to the scientific literature in this area." (Journal of Psychoactive Drugs)*

Addiction Treatment Matching: Research Foundations of the American Society of Addiction Medicine (ASAM) Criteria

David R. Gastfriend, MD
Editor

Addiction Treatment Matching: Research Foundations of the American Society of Addiction Medicine (ASAM) Criteria has been co-published simultaneously as *Journal of Addictive Diseases*, Volume 22, Supplement Number 1 2003.

The Haworth Medical Press®
An Imprint of The Haworth Press, Inc.

New York • London • Victoria (AU)
www.HaworthPress.com

Published by

The Haworth Medical Press®, 10 Alice Street, Binghamton, NY 13904-1580 USA

The Haworth Medical Press® is an imprint of The Haworth Press, Inc., 10 Alice Street, Binghamton, NY 13904-1580 USA.

Addiction Treatment Matching: Research Foundations of the American Society of Addiction Medicine (ASAM) Criteria has been co-published simultaneously as *Journal of Addictive Diseases*, Volume 22, Supplement Number 1 2003.

Cover design by Brooke Stiles

Library of Congress Cataloging-in-Publication Data

Addiction treatment matching : research foundations of the American Society of Addiction Medicine (asam) criteria / [edited by] David R. Gastfriend.
      p. cm.
   Includes bibliographical references and index.
     ISBN 0-7890-2429-2 (hard cover : alk. paper)–ISBN 0-7890-2430-6 (soft cover : alk. paper)
     1. Substance abuse–Treatment. I. Gastfriend, David R. II. American Society of Addiction Medicine. III. Journal of Addictive diseases.
RC564.A2913 2003
616.86′06–dc22
                                           2003022558

Indexing, Abstracting & Website/Internet Coverage

This section provides you with a list of major indexing & abstracting services. That is to say, each service began covering this periodical during the year noted in the right column. Most Websites which are listed below have indicated that they will either post, disseminate, compile, archive, cite or alert their own Website users with research-based content from this work. (This list is as current as the copyright date of this publication.)

Abstracting, Website/Indexing Coverage . . . . Year When Coverage Began

- *Abstracts in Anthropology* **1991**
- *ADDICTION ABSTRACTS*
    <http://www.tandf.co.uk/addiction-abs> **1994**
- *AgeLine Database* **2000**
- *Behavioral Medicine Abstracts* **1996**
- *Biosciences Information Service of Biological Abstracts*
    (BIOSIS) <http://www.biosis.org> **1983**
- *Cambridge Scientific Abstracts (Health & Safety Science*
    Abstracts/Risk Abstracts/Toxicology Abstracts)
    <http://www.csa.com> **1983**
- *Child Development Abstracts & Bibliography (in print & online)*
    <http://www.ukans.edu> **1982**
- *CINAHL (Cumulative Index to Nursing & Allied Health*
    Literature) <http://www.cinahl.com> **2000**
- *CNPIEC Reference Guide: Chinese National Directory*
    of Foreign Periodicals **1995**
- *Criminal Justice Abstracts* **1982**
- *Criminal Justice Periodical Index* **1983**
- *Current Contents/Social & Behavioral Sciences*
    <http://www.isinet.com> **1991**

(continued)

(continued)

Exact start date to come.

Special Bibliographic Notes related to special journal issues (separates) and indexing/abstracting:

- indexing/abstracting services in this list will also cover material in any "separate" that is co-published simultaneously with Haworth's special thematic journal issue or DocuSerial. Indexing/abstracting usually covers material at the article/chapter level.
- monographic co-editions are intended for either non-subscribers or libraries which intend to purchase a second copy for their circulating collections.
- monographic co-editions are reported to all jobbers/wholesalers/approval plans. The source journal is listed as the "series" to assist the prevention of duplicate purchasing in the same manner utilized for books-in-series.
- to facilitate user/access services all indexing/abstracting services are encouraged to utilize the co-indexing entry note indicated at the bottom of the first page of each article/chapter/contribution.
- this is intended to assist a library user of any reference tool (whether print, electronic, online, or CD-ROM) to locate the monographic version if the library has purchased this version but not a subscription to the source journal.
- individual articles/chapters in any Haworth publication are also available through the Haworth Document Delivery Service (HDDS).

Addiction Treatment Matching: Research Foundations of the American Society of Addiction Medicine (ASAM) Criteria

CONTENTS

ABOUT THE EDITOR

David R. Gastfriend, MD, is Director of the Addiction Research Program at Massachusetts General Hospital and Associate Professor of Psychiatry at Harvard Medical School. He founded the Fellowship in Addiction Psychiatry at the hospital and continues to teach and provide outpatient substance abuse clinical care. He is Chair of the Treatment Outcome Research Committee of the American Society of Addiction Medicine (ASAM), is a two-team elected Delegate-at Large on ASAM's Board, and also sits on the Board of the International Society of Addiction Medicine.

Dr. Gastfriend is co-editor of the leading book on treatment matching in the field, *The ASAM Patient Placement Criteria for Substance Abuse Disorders.* He is Associate Editor of the *Journal of Technology in Human Services* and serves on the editorial boards of the *Journal of Substance Abuse Treatment* and the *Journal of Addictive Diseases.* In 2001, he was the recipient of a five-year Mid-Career Investigator Award for Patient-Oriented Research from the National Institute on Drug Abuse (NIDA). Dr. Gastfriend is recognized for his work on implementing addictions placement criteria by provider networks, insurers, and state, federal, and international agencies.

Dr. Gastfriend has conducted studies of both pharmacologic and behavioral treatments of alcohol and drug use disorders. He initiated the first multi-site study to validate and refine the Patient Placement Criteria published by the ASAM funded by NIDA. Dr. Gastfriend is a former Co-Principal Investigator on NIDA's Cocaine Collaborative Psychotherapy Study and the National Institute on Alcohol Abuse and Alcoholism's collaborative study COMBINE. In COMBINE, he chaired the Assessment Committee and the Publications and Analysis Committee.

Foreword

There have been substantial changes over the past fifteen years in the way addiction treatment is delivered. Specifically, there has been a significant movement from treatment in primarily residential settings to predominantly outpatient care. As recently as the past decade, over 60% of substance abuse treatments were delivered in some form of residential (hospital or non-hospital) care.[1] By 1996 about 60% of addiction treatment programs were outpatient[1,2] and by 2002, more than 85% of all substance abuse treatment was provided in an outpatient setting.[3]

Why did this happen? Has there been an incremental improvement in the "technology of addiction treatment" as there has been in many medical procedures (e.g., laser surgery) such that what had previously taken months of intensive, residential care, now is able to be accomplished in less than 20 days of outpatient care? Has the impact of contemporary group counseling become so concentrated that patients can now get insights and understanding from two groups per week that used to take months of "two-a-days?" Any cursory examination of the contemporary treatment scene dispels these ideas immediately.[4]

In fact, what happened is that over a fifteen year period much of healthcare management was concerned primarily with costs rather than outcomes; and this influence was able to almost completely eliminate the use of the full continuum of care in the treatment of addiction. In turn, this was possible because of many factors (stigma, perverse incentives, capitated contracts, etc.) but particularly the absence of evidence that the continuum of care was necessary for recovery from the illnesses of alcoholism and drug dependence. In fact, the drafting of the initial version of the Patient Placement Criteria (PPC) by the American Soci-

[Haworth co-indexing entry note]: "Foreword." McLellan, A. Thomas. Co-published simultaneously in *Journal of Addictive Diseases* (The Haworth Medical Press, an imprint of The Haworth Press, Inc.) Vol. 22, Supplement No. 1, 2003, pp. xv-xviii; and: *Addiction Treatment Matching: Research Foundations of the American Society of Addiction Medicine (ASAM) Criteria* (ed: David R. Gastfriend) The Haworth Medical Press, an imprint of The Haworth Press, Inc., 2003, pp. xv-xviii. Single or multiple copies of this article are available for a fee from The Haworth Document Delivery Service [1-800-HAWORTH, 9:00 a.m. - 5:00 p.m. (EST). E-mail address: docdelivery@haworthpress.com].

http://www.haworthpress.com/store/product.asp?sku=J069
xv

ety of Addiction Medicine (ASAM) can reasonably be credited with slowing and in some cases preventing the deterioration in the care delivery system. Who knows what the addiction treatment infrastructure would look like today had ASAM not stepped forward?

However, the initial power of the ASAM-PPC contribution was driven by its intuitive, face validity, its clinical common sense and the political power of a prominent and respected physician group–not by an empirically derived, scientifically validated algorithm supporting that construct. In the years since the drafting and implementation of the ASAM-PPC, there have been many studies supporting the basic elements of the placement process and adding refinements to improve it. However, this volume of work offers the most significant, comprehensive and broadly useful set of studies testing the reliability, validity and utility of the American Society of Addiction Medicine (ASAM) Patient Placement Criteria. As such, the volume and the individual studies within it will likely be among the most important, practical contributions to the treatment of addiction for a long while.

Because the ASAM-PPC are now a standard part of contemporary substance abuse treatment, it is easy to overlook the basic contributions made by ASAM and particularly through the work of Gastfriend, Mee-Lee, Sharon and others. Here I list some that are so obvious now that their historical contribution may not be appreciated.

- *The type of setting and program in which a substance-dependent patient is initially placed makes a measurable difference in their length of stay and their eventual outcomes.*

While, this simple statement seems obvious, it was not obvious to the many managed care organizations that have taken a "fail outpatient first" approach to care management. Again, without empirical evidence refuting this dogma it was not easy or even possible to mount a winning clinical argument. The data from this volume are quite significant and provide substantial justification for use of the full continuum of care.

- *The clinical recommendation regarding what is likely to be the best type of setting and program for a patient is not simply an intuitive or experiential determination–but rather a reproducible and logical process.*

Although it is clear that the ASAM-PPC will continue to evolve and there is likely to be greater use of computer algorithms, it is important to note that from the first iteration of the criteria, there has been a clear, face valid logic to the process. Perhaps the most significant development in the PPC over the years has been the effort to standardize the data requirements and the data definitions for the elements that go into the placement algorithm. Like most other areas of medical science, this has transformed what used to be a craft into a procedure that can be transported and reproduced with reliability and validity. That the ASAM has made these criteria public and available for scrutiny and study is also laudable–again, in an historical context where many managed care organizations have kept their own recipes for patient placement secret and removed from scientific evaluation.

One observation follows from these first two points. Since there is mounting evidence for reliability, validity and reproducibility in the ASAM-PPC "procedure"; and since there is additional evidence that this "procedure" is clinically important to the eventual outcome and costs of an episode of substance abuse treatment–it follows that ASAM-PPC procedures should have a legitimate procedure code and should be a recognized and reimbursed part of substance abuse treatment. This is already the case in some states and healthcare organizations–but it is not standard practice yet. In turn, the ability to perform this procedure properly should be something that is taught as a standard part of clinical training for caregivers in our field.

- *ASAM-PPC placement decisions do not always lead to significant lengths of stay nor favorable outcomes.*

This too is expectable and obvious. However, I think it is important to note that with the availability of standard criteria, standard data collection and a validated algorithm, there is now opportunity to examine the remaining sources of potential error in the patient placement/ engagement process. Without the availability of these standardized elements–it never would be possible to improve the process. Indeed, the greater standardization and validation of the ASAM-PPC will enable opportunities to study several of the important remaining elements. For example, one significant source of variance already identified is the variability of amount and types of services within each of the levels of care. If a Level III treatment program is not actually providing the requisite services for that level it could be an important factor in accounting for some lack of engagement and retention and even poor outcomes.

In conclusion, ASAM should be congratulated on not just inventing and supporting the Patient Placement Criteria–but especially for subjecting those criteria to the type of rigorous, parametric study represented by the papers in this volume. The findings here and elsewhere have done much to substantiate the clinically sensible algorithm and process developed by the original authors of the ASAM-PPC. Beyond that contribution to contemporary treatment, these studies point the way for a next generation of studies that promise greater insights into the factors that control a patient's decision to enter care, the type of care that is best for them, and the factors that affect early engagement and subsequent retention in that care. The addiction field has benefited already from this body of work and there is every indication that the ASAM studies of the future will provide even more insights and benefits.

A. Thomas McLellan
Treatment Research Institute
600 Public Ledger Building
150 South Independence Mall (West)
Philadelphia, PA 19106

REFERENCES

1. Substance Abuse and Mental Health Services Administration (SAMHSA). *Uniform Facility Data Set (UFDS): Data for 1996 and 1980-1996* (DHHS Publication No. SMA 98-3176). Washington, DC: U.S. Government Printing Office.

2. McKusick D, Mark T, Edward D, Harwood HR, Buck J, DiLeonardo J, Genuardi J. Spending for mental health and substance abuse treatment. *Health Affairs.* 1998; 17(5):147-157.

3. Substance Abuse and Mental Health Services Administration (SAMHSA). *National Survey of Substance Abuse Treatment (NSSAT): Data for 2000 and 2001* (DHHS Publication No. SMA 98-3176). Washington, DC: U.S. Government Printing Office.

4. McLellan AT, Carise D, Kleber HD. The national addiction treatment infrastructure: Can it support the public's demand for quality care? *J. Substance Abuse Treatment.* 2003;25:117-121.

EDITORIAL

The ASAM Patient Placement Criteria: Context, Concepts and Continuing Development

David R. Gastfriend, MD
David Mee-Lee, MD

David R. Gastfriend is Director, Addiction Research Program, Massachusetts General Hospital and Associate Professor of Psychiatry, Harvard Medical School, Boston, MA.

David Mee-Lee is Chair, ASAM Criteria Committee and Coalition for National Clinical Criteria; Training and Consulting, Davis, CA.

Address correspondence to: David R. Gastfriend, MD, Director, Addiction Research Program, Massachusetts General Hospital, 388 Commonwealth Avenue, Lower Level, Boston, MA 02115 (E-mail: DGastfriend@Partners.org).

[Haworth co-indexing entry note]: "The ASAM Patient Placement Criteria: Context, Concepts and Continuing Development." Gastfriend, David R., and David Mee-Lee. Co-published simultaneously in *Journal of Addictive Diseases* (The Haworth Medical Press, an imprint of The Haworth Press, Inc.) Vol. 22, Supplement No. 1, 2003, pp. 1-8; and: *Addiction Treatment Matching: Research Foundations of the American Society of Addiction Medicine (ASAM) Criteria* (ed: David R. Gastfriend) The Haworth Medical Press, an imprint of The Haworth Press, Inc., 2003, pp. 1-8. Single or multiple copies of this article are available for a fee from The Haworth Document Delivery Service [1-800-HAWORTH, 9:00 a.m. - 5:00 p.m. (EST). E-mail address: docdelivery@haworthpress.com].

1

A decade after publication, the *Patient Placement Criteria (PPC)* published by the American Society of Addiction Medicine (ASAM) has become a national model for addiction care, bringing order to a field in turmoil. Technology has given the PPC adequate reliability, feasibility, and resolution. An independent Center for Substance Abuse Treatment panel found sufficient face validity to recommend that states proceed with implementation and evaluation. Controlled studies described in this volume find evidence for validity using a comprehensive computerized implementation of the PPC in over 1,000 uninsured, Medicaid, privately insured and Veterans Administration patients. Both naturalistic and randomized trials indicate that PPC matching was associated with less morbidity, better function, or less service utilization than mis-matching to lower level of care. Challenges remain, including low resolution of decision rules and poor reliability in site characterization. The new millennium brings improved software that should empower community programs to join this research.

Although treatment for addictive disorders is effective, no single treatment is appropriate for all individuals.[1-3] Many programs impose a single treatment model or level-of-care (LOC) on all patients. Meanwhile, a predominantly short-term cost focus leads managed care to limit care. The American Society of Addiction Medicine's Patient Placement Criteria for the Treatment of Substance-Related Disorders (ASAM PPC) evolved from earlier efforts[4,5] to help clinicians and payers use LOCs in a rational and individualized way that was ideology-blind, clinically driven, outcomes-oriented, and oriented along a continuum of care.[6]

Research data are badly needed to drive the evolution of the ASAM Criteria. In the continuing series of PPC-1,[7] PPC-2,[8] and PPC-2R,[9] development is analogous to that of the American Psychiatric Association's Diagnostic and Statistical Manual of Mental Disorders (DSM-IV), which is now in its fifth version–a work in progress.[10] The data-driven process will take the scientific documentation of PPC beyond the status of consensus treatment guidelines[11] and beyond the recent spate of hypothetical critiques.[12,13] There is already a consensus endorsement of the face validity of the ASAM PPC from a comprehensive independent review undertaken by CSAT in 1995.[13] The research literature in general provides extensive support for the principle of PPC multidimensional needs assessment in treatment planning.[14-16] By the year 2000, numerous studies have shown that constructs such as the PPC dimensions and levels of care predict treatment success and cost effectiveness.[17-21] More directly, considerable research now exists on the PPC itself as a treatment planning methodology. At this time, there are seven known studies of the ASAM PPC, with over seven million dollars of funding from three federal agencies, including the National Institute on Drug Abuse, the National Institute on Alcohol Abuse and Alcoholism, and the Center for Substance Abuse Treatment. This volume indicates that several methodologic challenges to placement criteria have been put to the test.

Can Programs Be Characterized According to Level-of-Care? The study in this volume by Levine et al.[22] used two methods to gather different but equally vital information: a quantitative questionnaire of staffing/services and a qualitative evaluation of program activities/atmosphere. Although there was adequate inter-level distinction (i.e., between Level II and III), high intra-level variance (i.e., within Level II programs) was problematic and will cause noise in PPC trials and risk artifactual differences in research outcomes. Detailed standards will be needed for future research and program certification.

Are the PPC Feasible? In printed form, the intricate hierarchical steps in PPC assessment and decision-making make for poor feasibility. Also, abbreviated one- or two-page adaptations offer poor reliability. Nevertheless, feasibility was suggested when a one-page tabular PPC-1 adaptation for the Boston Target Cities project was associated with 38% greater likelihood to transition from detoxification to continuing treatment within 30 days (odds ratio = 1.55, p < .005) and significantly less detoxification again within 90 days (odds ratio = .57, p < .005) compared to conventional direct admission without criteria.[23]

Morey applied an abbreviated PPC-1 algorithm retrospectively to telephone survey data.[24] This algorithm yielded a good degree of face validity and also utilization patterns that suggested concurrent validity (Morey, L, personal communication). McKay et al. found predictive validity only for some aspects of dependence, but used a retrospective partial implementation of only the psychosocial (not biomedical) dimensions of the PPC-1.[25] Deck et al. report in this volume that, with greater training and formal brief PPC-1 implementation, Oregon realized greater individualization of length of stay and increased utilization of the innovative Level II services than Washington state.[26] But the lack of an adequate, comprehensive, and feasible methodology has confounded researchers and end-users alike.[27,28] In a 1998 adaptation of PPC-1 in West Virginia, even with extensive training noted that " . . . ability to determine . . . a particular level of care is . . . difficult due to (a) long and often ambiguous text/format . . . and (b) the lack of clear directions . . ."[27]

Can the PPC Be Standardized? Given the intricate PPC branching logic, Gastfriend[6,16,21] first developed a computerized approach to facilitate a comprehensive structured interview and scoring algorithm for the PPC. Using the microcomputer to present the counselor with a sequence of research-validated questions to ask the patient, and then score the counselor's input in real-time, the researchers were able to achieve an average duration of administration of less than 60 minutes per patient in a large public sector cohort.[28] The paper in this volume by Baker et al.,[29] demonstrates good inter-rater reliability for the PPC-1 instrument (intraclass correlation coefficient = 0.77). This method has now been tested in three prospective studies.[30-32] Staines et al.[31] report the concurrent validity results of a New York City naturalistic study using this computerized algorithm in 248 newly admitted, primarily alcohol dependent subjects. The results find areas of agreement as well as disagreement between the algorithm and clinicians, and more importantly, pave the methodologic path for empirical revision of PPC to yield increasing precision.

Can the PPC Be Validated? In a predictive validity analysis of the same dataset described by Staines et al.,[31] Magura et al.[32] show that outpatients who were receiving a lower LOC than recommended by the PPC-1 had substantially and significantly ($p < 0.01$) more days of alcohol use at 3-months than those who were correctly matched to treatment. Using either of two methods, computer-scoring or clinician scoring, the results were significant, even after controlling for baseline severity and the effect of LOC itself, although the computer-scoring sharpened these group differences (adjusted mean days of alcohol use in past 30 for match vs. mismatched groups: computer-scored = 2.7 vs. 8.3; clinician-scored = 4.2 vs. 9.2).

In another naturalistic study of 95 VA patients near Boston, Massachusetts, PPC-1 matching was associated with reduced hospital service utilization.[30] Male veterans who received Level III (residential) care but who were scored by the PPC-1 algorithm as needing the more intensive Level IV (hospital level) care utilized nearly twice as many hospital bed days over the subsequent year as those who were scored as needing only Levels II (e.g., day treatment) or III (e.g., residential) care ($p < .05$). This result was not associated with differential chronicity prior to the index admission (p = n.s.). Finally, both Magura et al.[32] and Sharon et al.[30] failed to find any clinical advantage from over-matching.

The first randomized controlled trial of placement criteria to date is a multi-site study by Gastfriend et al. in central, eastern, and northern Massachusetts. In this project, the PPC-1 algorithm has been previously reported to show good concurrent validity.[28] Preliminary analysis of 700 subjects who were randomly either matched or mismatched to Level II or III treatment, suggests that patients with inadequate LOC had significantly higher no-show rates.[33]

As demonstrated by the papers in this volume, more than one study now indicates some degree of predictive validity for the ASAM-PPC.[30,32] This replication of concurrent and predictive findings by different investigators using different outcome variables in different populations is a milestone. The body of work contained in this volume demonstrates that the ASAM-PPC is a treatment matching methodology whose time has come.

What Is Needed for Further Development? Revisions will require additional analysis of existing data, new studies, and new study techniques. Definitive analysis from the largest data set is still pending. One detailed analysis from this study of a single dimension, Relapse/Continued Use Potential, as described in this volume by Gastfriend et al.[34] finds important methodologic artifacts, which decision analysis can resolve, improving validity. New construct development may further improve reliability and validity. The PPC-2R is ready for studies of the relevance and validity of its dual diagnosis determinations, which now specify in detail both services and patient needs, as described by the paper in this volume by Minkoff et al.[35] Subsequent studies should be designed to permit analysis at greater resolution of detail in both service characterization and needs assessment so that particular dimensions and even discrete decision rules can be subjected to outcome analysis and revised. A key artifact in current studies is the high rate of dropout in public and insured samples. Placement criteria will require field-testing, without the constraints of the narrow subject selection common in university-based efficacy studies. If placement criteria are to be credible, they will need to be sufficiently robust to yield significant results despite the confounds of real-world subject samples and treatment programs. The availability of new, ASAM-authorized, user-friendly assessment software for the PPC-2R will permit wide-scale distribution among treatment centers. This end-user software will include built-in capability for web-enabled, confidential, data uploading. This opens an enormous opportunity for naturalistic effectiveness trials in non-academic treatment programs. The papers in this volume demonstrate the achievements of placement criteria that have accrued through more than a decade of consensus generation, evaluation, pilot testing, methods development, psychometric study, and controlled research. Publication of this first volume of papers on the ASAM Criteria establishes a knowledge foundation to support a new architecture for the information technology of substance disorder treatment. Scientists have begun the crucial process of testing the current expert consensus product, but future work will require a national network of data gathering, quantitative analysis, and feedback.

AUTHORS NOTE

This work on the validity and continuing development of the ASAM Criteria owes special thanks to the following people whose contributions were essential to its preparation: Dennis McCarty, PhD, A. Thomas McLellan, PhD, and Bruce Rounsaville, MD, for guidance on design and interpretation; Larry Muenz, PhD, for statistical design; Jennifer Bassett, BA, Eugenia Conde-Dudding, BA, Olga Gurevich, MA, Donna Janas, MA, LICMH, Marc Korczykowski, BA, Mark Morin, BA, John Riordan, BA, Kingsley Turner, BA, and Jennifer Vickers, MA, for the care of subjects and data collection; and Kara Bjornberg, BA, Mara Larson, BA, Emerson Moses, BA, Sandrine Pirard, MD, Christine Quirk, and Natasha Zebrowski for editorial support.

Supported by Grants # R01-DA08781 and K24-DA00427 to Dr. Gastfriend from the National Institute on Drug Abuse.

This article is based on a paper presented at the 32nd Annual Medical-Scientific Conference, American Society of Addiction Medicine, April 20, 2001, Century City, Los Angeles, CA.

REFERENCES

1. Institute of Medicine. Broadening the base of treatment for alcohol problems. Washington: National Academy Press, 1990.

2. Leshner AI. Science-based views of drug addiction and its treatment. JAMA. 1999;282:1314-1381.

3. Principles of drug addiction treatment–a research-based guide. Principles of effective treatment. National Institutes of Health Publication, no. 99-4180, 1999.

4. Hoffmann NG, Halikas JA, Mee-Lee D. The Cleveland admission, discharge, and transfer criteria: model for chemical dependency treatment programs. Cleveland: Northern Ohio Chemical Dependency Treatment Directors Association, 1987.

5. Weedman RD. Admission, continued stay and discharge criteria for adult alcoholism and drug dependence treatment services. Irvine: National Association of Addiction Treatment Providers, 1987.

6. Gastfriend D. Patient placement criteria. In: Galanter M, Kleber HD, eds. Textbook of substance abuse treatment. Washington: The American Psychiatric Press, 1999:121-127.

7. Hoffmann N, Halikas J, Mee-Lee D, Weedman R. American society of addiction medicine–patient placement criteria for the treatment of psychoactive substance use disorders. Washington, DC: American Society of Addiction Medicine, Inc., 1991.

8. American Society of Addiction Medicine. Patient placement criteria for the treatment of substance-related disorders. Chevy Chase: American Society of Addiction Medicine, Inc., 1996.

9. Mee-Lee D, Shulman GD, Fishman M et al., eds. ASAM patient placement criteria for the treatment of substance-related disorders, second edition-revised (ASAM PPC-2R). Chevy Chase: American Society of Addiction Medicine, Inc., 2001.

10. American Psychiatric Association: DSM-IV diagnostic and statistical manual of mental disorders, fourth edition. Washington: American Psychiatric Press, 1994.

11. American Psychiatric Association. Practice guideline for treatment of patients with substance use disorders: alcohol, cocaine, opioids. Washington: American Psychiatric Association, 1995.

12. Book J, Harbim H, Marques C et al. The ASAM's and Green Spring's alcohol and drug detoxification and rehabilitation criteria for utilization review. Am J Addiction. 1995;4:187-197.

13. Center for Substance Abuse Treatment. The role and current status of patient placement criteria in the treatment of substance use disorders. Treatment improvement protocol (TIP). Rockville: Substance Abuse and Mental Health Services Administration, 1995.

14. Hser YI, Polinsky ML, Maglione M, Anglin MD. Matching clients' needs with drug treatment services. J Subst Abuse Treat. 1999;16:299-305.

15. McLellan AT, Grissom GR, Zanis D et al. Problem-service 'matching' in addiction treatment: a prospective study in 4 programs. Arch Gen Psychiatry. 1997;54:730-735.

16. Gastfriend DR, Lu SH, Sharon E. Placement matching: challenges and technical progress. Subst Use Misuse. 2000;35:2191-213.

17. Annis H. Patient-treatment matching in the management of alcoholism. NIDA Res Monogr. 1988;90:152-161.

18. Hayashida M, Alterman AI, McLellan AT et al. Comparative effectiveness and costs of inpatient and outpatient detoxification of patients with mild-to-moderate alcohol withdrawal syndrome. N Engl J Med. 1989;320:358-365.

19. Alterman AI, O'Brien CP, McLellan AT et al. Effectiveness and costs of inpatient versus day hospital cocaine rehabilitation. J Nerv Mental Dis. 1994;182:157-163.

20. Mechanic D, Schlesinger M, McAlpine DD. Management of mental health and substance abuse services: state of the art an early results. Milbank Q. 1995;73:19-55.

21. Gastfriend DR, McLellan AT. Treatment matching: theoretic basis and practical implications. Med Clin N Amer. 1997;81:945-966.

22. Levine HJ, Turner W, Reif S et al. Determining service variations between and within ASAM Levels of Care. J Addict Dis. 2003; 22(Suppl. 1):9-25.

23. Plough A, Shirley L, Zaremba N et al. CSAT target cities demonstration final evaluation report. Boston: Office for Treatment Improvement, 1996.

24. Morey L. Patient placement criteria: linking typologies to managed care. Alcohol Health and Research World. 1996;20:36-44.

25. McKay JR, Cacciola JS, McLellan AT et al. An initial evaluation of the psychosocial dimensions of the american society of addiction medicine criteria for inpatient vs. intensive outpatient substance abuse rehabilitation. J Stud Alcohol. 1997; 58:239-252.

26. Deck D, Gabriel R, Knudsen J, Grams G. Impact of patient placement criteria on substance abuse treatment under the Oregon Health Plan. J Addict Dis. 2003; 22(Suppl. 1):27-44.

27. May WW. A field application of the ASAM placement criteria in a 12-step model of treatment for chemical dependency. J Addict. Dis. 1998;17:77-91.

28. Turner WM, Turner KH, Reif S et al. Feasibility of multidimensional substance abuse treatment matching: Automating the ASAM patient placement criteria. Drug Alcohol Depend. 1999;55:35-43.

29. Baker SL, Gastfriend DR. Reliability of multidimensional substance abuse treatment matching: implementing the ASAM patient placement criteria. J Addict Dis. 2003; 22(Suppl. 1):45-60.

30. Sharon E, Krebs C, Turner W et al. Predictive validity of the ASAM patient placement criteria for hospital utilization. J Addict Dis. 2003; 22(Suppl. 1): 79-93.

31. Staines G, Kosanke N, Magura S et al. Convergent validity of the ASAM patient placement criteria using a standardized computer algorithm. J Addict Dis. 2003; 22(Suppl. 1):61-77.

32. Magura S, Staines G, Kosanke N et al. Predictive validity of the ASAM patient placement criteria: outcomes for patients naturalistically matched and mismatched to levels of care. J Subst Abuse Treatment. Am J Addict. 2003; 12:386-397.

33. Gastfriend DR. ASAM annual medical-scientific meeting. Los Angeles: April 2001.

34. Gastfriend DR, Rubin A, Sharon E et al. New constructs and assessments for relapse and continued use potential in the ASAM patent placement criteria. J Addict Dis. 2003; 22(Suppl. 1):95-111.

35. Minkoff K, Zweben J, Rosenthal R, Ries R. Development of service intensity criteria and program categories for individuals with co-occurring disorders. J Addict Dis. 2003; 22(Suppl. 1):113-129.

Determining Service Variations Between and Within ASAM Levels of Care

Helen J. Levine, PhD
Winston Turner, PhD
Sharon Reif, BA
Donna Janas, BA
David R. Gastfriend, MD

SUMMARY. The American Society of Addiction Medicine (ASAM) Criteria Validity Study at Massachusetts General Hospital and Harvard Medical School randomized patients between programs in two levels of care. It therefore became critical to determine the extent to which programs met ASAM level of care (LOC) descriptions. Quantitative sur-

Helen J. Levine is affiliated with JSI Research & Training, Inc., Boston, MA, and Schneider Institute of Health Policy, Heller School of Health Policy, Brandeis University.

Winston Turner, Donna Janas, and David R. Gastfriend are affiliated with the Addiction Research Program, Departments of Psychiatry, Massachusetts General Hospital and Harvard Medical School.

Sharon Reif is affiliated with the Schneider Institute of Health Policy, Heller School of Health Policy, Brandeis University, and the Addiction Research Program, Departments of Psychiatry, Massachusetts General Hospital and Harvard Medical School.

Address correspondence to: David R. Gastfriend, MD, Director, Addiction Research Program, Massachusetts General Hospital, 388 Commonwealth Avenue, Lower Level, Boston, MA 02115 (E-mail: DGastfriend @Partners.org).

Supported by Grants # R01-DA08781 and K24-DA00427 to Dr. Gastfriend from the National Institute on Drug Abuse.

[Haworth co-indexing entry note]: "Determining Service Variations Between and Within ASAM Levels of Care." Levine, Helen J. et al. Co-published simultaneously in *Journal of Addictive Diseases* (The Haworth Medical Press, an imprint of The Haworth Press, Inc.) Vol. 22, Supplement No. 1, 2003, pp. 9-25; and: *Addiction Treatment Matching: Research Foundations of the American Society of Addiction Medicine (ASAM) Criteria* (ed: David R. Gastfriend) The Haworth Medical Press, an imprint of The Haworth Press, Inc., 2003, pp. 9-25. Single or multiple copies of this article are available for a fee from The Haworth Document Delivery Service [1-800-HAWORTH, 9:00 a.m. - 5:00 p.m. (EST). E-mail address: docdelivery@haworthpress.com].

Digital Object Identifier: 10.1300/J069v22S01_02

veys (checklist) and qualitative case studies (field observation, key informant interviews) documented care variation within and between two ASAM LOCs in 12 substance abuse treatment units. These LOCs were: Level II (Intensive Outpatient Treatment) and Level III (Medically Monitored Residential Treatment). The Level II and Level III programs, as a group, met ASAM LOC criteria, but data showed major within-level variation by hours per day and number and type of skilled treatment services. Observational data suggest considerable within-level variation due to managed care and staff training. In multi-site PPC validity studies, it will be crucial to examine within-LOC variation and take into account payment sources and staff training when assessing patient outcomes. *[Article copies available for a fee from The Haworth Document Delivery Service: 1-800-HAWORTH. E-mail address: <docdelivery@haworthpress.com> Website: <http://www.HaworthPress.com> © 2003 by The Haworth Press, Inc. All rights reserved.]*

KEYWORDS. ASAM levels of care, qualitative study, managed care, staff training

INTRODUCTION

Managed care has become a predominant influence in the organization and delivery of substance abuse treatment. Managed care organization (MCOs) rely upon assessment protocols for appropriate patient placement in care that meets the twin goals of effective and efficient care delivery.[1] Among the protocols developed by both providers and MCOs, the most common of the patient placement protocols has been published by the American Society of Addiction Medicine (ASAM).[2]

The Patient Placement Criteria (PPC), published by ASAM, established via consensus a hierarchy of treatment settings, i.e., levels of care (LOC), and defined these in quantitative terms.[3] What is unclear from the published descriptions of the ASAM LOCs is how treatment really differs between and within LOC. The ASAM Criteria Validity Study at Massachusetts General Hospital and Harvard Medical School randomized patients between two LOCs, Level II (Intensive Outpatient) and Level III (Medically Monitored Inpatient), according to ASAM match or mismatch status.[4-6] To assess LOC validity of treatment assignment in the study, it became a critical concern for the project to determine the extent to which a program actually fulfilled the LOC description. This question is crucial for effective implementation of the ASAM Criteria in community treatment programs, too; it has existed since the original publication (PPC-1) in 1991,[2] through the 1996 second edition (PPC-2),[7] and persists in the second edition, revised (PPC-2R) published in 2001.[8] If programs cannot be reliably characterized, it will be difficult or impossible to achieve the clinical improvements and cost savings that are promised by placement criteria matching.

Researchers typically have used checklists that provide a quantitative review of objective descriptors, such as hours of programming or presence of medical staff. But these data may not tell the whole story. To obtain a complementary perspective, qualitative contextual data also need to be gathered. Any differences that either contradict the basic distinctions between levels or document homogeneity within levels would be important for studies of PPC and would potentially have broader implications for dissemination of PPC and managed care. For example, if no differences were found between two LOCs, there would be little support for differential cost. Alternatively, if substantial differences were found within a single LOC, the validity of the level definition would come into question and similar reimbursement rates would appear to be inappropriate. Finally, such findings would raise questions as to whether such differences arose due to patient severity, treatment setting, staff training, payer mix, or other provider incentives.

The increase in the number of MCOs offering substance abuse treatment services has dramatically changed the array of types of care, services offered, and reimbursement mechanisms throughout the system.[1,2] As new emphasis is being placed on a variety of programs of varying levels of intensity, treatment settings are expanding LOCs to provide more treatment options for clients. While traditional quantitative facility surveys still can give an overview of the system, the accelerating rate of system change cannot be completely captured through standardized surveys.[9] More dynamic data collection methods are called for to describe the far-reaching and complex changes in service delivery and overall organization of the treatment system.

In this project, case studies of 12 substance abuse treatment units were constructed in 1995 and in 1997, using both quantitative survey data and qualitative observational data. Data were gathered regarding the setting of care, staff education, services provided, payer sources, and treatment duration. The LOC descriptions were specifically examined for the PPC-1, however given the consistency of the major levels of care across PPC-2 and PPC-2R, the study goals and methods apply equally well to these later editions. In fact, given the expansion of sub-levels in the PPC-2 and PPC-2R editions and their requisite increased specificity, it becomes even more important to determine service variations between and within ASAM LOCs.

METHODS

Field research is particularly suited to describing sensitive social interactions under conditions of change.[10] Social scientists have conducted field observation studies in substance abuse and mental health treatment settings for more than 40 years.[11,12] Observation studies are conducted under naturalistic conditions, in contrast to randomized designs, which may raise ethical, legal, and political dilemmas and may not reflect real world influences on treatment outcomes.[13] Ethnographic research captures richer detail about the context in which treatment takes place.[14,15] This study uses both qualitative and quantitative data to examine treatment conditions as they exist in practice, and to uncover differences and similarities between and within ASAM LOCs.

Descriptions of Levels of Care

The study design for this project consisted of a field observation study of ASAM Level II intensive outpatient treatment units (i.e., partial hospital/day treatment) and ASAM Level III medically monitored (i.e., non-hospital) residential substance abuse treatment units. This services variability study was preliminary to the ASAM Criteria Validity Study at Massachusetts General Hospital, which concentrated on levels II and III, given the important cost differential between these two levels, ethical obstacles to randomizing level IV hospital patients to lower levels of care, and feasibility challenges of attempting to randomize level I outpatients to more intensive treatments. The descriptions of levels II and III used for this study were published in the first edition of the ASAM PPC (PPC1). This edition provides the prototypical levels II and III used in the subsequent PPC2 and PPC2-revised editions.

ASAM Level II Care: The ASAM PPC-1 established 4 treatment level characteristics and 16 programmatic requirements for Level II care. In summary, a Level II unit should have a structured program with a qualified staff that provides a minimum of 9 treatment hours per week. Services are correlated to patients' clinical needs. The patient interacts with a real world environment while supported by a structured therapeutic milieu. The Level II program includes the following: counseling contact at each visit, a minimum of 2 skilled treatment services for at least 3 days per week, 24-hour emergency telephone availability, a physical exam conducted by a physician at or soon after admission, individual biopsychosocial assessments, individual treatment plans that are reviewed at specified times, direct affiliation with more or less intensive LOCs, and an appropriate professional setting in a permanent facility.

ASAM Level III Care: In addition to the Level II requirements noted above, to meet ASAM PPC-1 description of a Level III unit, programs must have a planned regimen of 24-hour professionally directed evaluation, care, and treatment for addicted patients in an inpatient setting. A Level III unit must support services for detoxification, intensive inpatient addictions treatment, and conjoint treatment of coexisting biomedical and/or emotional or behavioral problems. The unit must have inpatient beds, in a permanent facility, a multidisciplinary staff, including a registered nurse, counseling staff, and a physician who is available by telephone 24 hours a day for patients receiving detoxification. Licensed staff must be available to administer medications in accordance with physician orders.

Programs in the ASAM Observational Study

Research assistants observed 9 programs, each for two weeks, in 1995. Some organizations operated more than one program. Researchers reviewed patient assessment instruments, viewed program activities, took extensive field notes, and conducted key informant interviews with patients, staff, and administrators. In addition, researchers surveyed administrators, using quantitative checklists documenting ASAM LOC attributes. At the end of the observation period, research assistants wrote 3-5 page summaries documenting how the ASAM PPC-1 descriptions of LOC for Levels II or III were operationalized in the treatment units. After initial training in field research techniques, the research assistants were supervised throughout their observation period and an experienced field researcher (HJL) reviewed field notes.

In 1997, research assistants revisited programs that continued in operation (5 remained active in the ASAM Criteria Validity Study) and also observed treatment at three new programs that had joined the ASAM Study, for a total of 12 program case studies. Although the study was designed for a limited sample size and no statistical analysis, the range of programs was thought to be representative of the state's offerings and the descriptive analysis was chosen to illustrate conceptual and practical needs for a developing methodology for LOC program specification.

RESULTS

1995 Site Visits. In 1995, participating Level II programs met ASAM criteria, by and large, but showed considerable diversity regarding the number and type of skilled treatment services offered, staff philosophy, duration of treatment, and payer sources. All programs were located in permanent facilities and had written treatment protocols, individual treatment plans, and 24-hour staff availability. All qualified for their respective LOCs according to the minimum program requirements set by the Massachusetts Bureau of Substance Abuse Services, which had adopted ASAM's LOC definitions prior to the study.

ASAM Level II Programs

Program II-a was located in a community hospital that offered all four levels of the ASAM continuum of care. Patients presented with a wide range of severity, and all patients were insured (indemnity, HMO). Interestingly, Level II patients received the same daily services as Level III patients, including a physical exam upon admission, monitoring of vital signs every shift change, daily individual counseling, and treatment groups. Groups operated from 8:30 a.m. to 4:30 p.m. Patients had 2 hours of free time in the afternoons but had to remain on the unit until 4:30 p.m. Several complained about being bored and having to stay in the unit even during their free time, when no programming was provided.

Program II-b. Located in a new building with a waterfront view, this Level II was notable for its comfortable atmosphere and beautiful physical environment. Staff members were relaxed and appeared to enjoy their work and working together. The Level II unit offered a 28-day private non-profit women's day program that mothers could attend with infants younger than 3 months. Mothers participated in groups from 9:15 a.m. to noon when other patients visited an AA meeting and had lunch outside the facility. Patients received individual counseling one day a week, and educational groups were offered several days a week. Counselors were licensed and were educated at the master's level or above.

Patients had access to both Level I and Level III care programs that served both genders and could be referred offsite to several Level III programs. There was a daily outpatient program (Level I) and a coed evening program (Level II) at the site. Female patients were referred back and forth between the day and evening programs. Other male and female patients participated in a court program staffed by 3 clinicians. On-site Social Security case managers monitored Supplemental Security Income (SSI) beneficiaries. In addition, the site had an extensive library with treatment materials and a prevention program that served city schools. Level I and Level II patients received similar services, but Level II patients spent more time in the facility and attended more groups.

The program served a diverse mix of patients; i.e., women, new mothers, men, court ordered clients, and SSI eligible patients. Except for the new mothers, however, there were no specific groups for special populations. Perhaps because of the relatively high level of education and licensing, staff could adapt group sessions to address issues relevant to members of these special populations.

Program II-c. Located on the grounds of a university medical center, this Level II program described itself as a structured substance abuse outpatient unit. It served 8-12 patients per day, Monday through Friday, 9 a.m.-3:30 p.m. Most patients attended no longer than 10 days. Many were uninsured, and their treatment was funded by the Massachusetts Department of Public Health, Bureau of Substance Abuse Services. The staff viewed the program either as an alternative to an affiliated inpatient unit (Level III) or a transition from inpatient care. Services included individual therapy, group therapy, outpatient detoxification, a dual diagnosis program, and educational programs. Staff exerted strong efforts to help patients examine their substance abuse behaviors, making some patients uncomfortable.

Though dedicated, staff members worried about understaffing, vacant positions, lack of community housing for aftercare options, lack of resources, and feelings of being overwhelmed. These concerns raised questions about the impact of staff stress on service delivery.

Program II-d. This Level II chemical dependency treatment unit was a relatively new for-profit program. The main payer was a managed care company. In operation for just under two years, the program had a small, master's level counseling staff and few patients. A nurse was available, and an addiction psychiatry fellow performed medical intakes and saw patients once a week. A senior psychiatrist supervised staff and was available to provide support. Although designed to treat up to a dozen people, no more than 3 patients were present any single day during the two-week observation period. The program provided intake assessments, offered psychodynamic group therapy, showed educational videos, and encouraged patients to attend 12-step program meetings daily.

This unit met ASAM Level II criteria, but it offered less intensive services than the other Level II programs described. For example, individual counseling was minimal. While there was a structured program, few specialized groups were offered, perhaps because of the low patient census. Patient attendance at the program appeared inconsistent and/or brief.

ASAM Level III Programs

Similar to the Level II units, the Level III units observed in 1995 met the ASAM criteria, but addiction treatment varied considerably across programs. The differences observed in patient length of stay and the number of skilled treatment services appeared to be due more to staff training and patient insurance or provider incentives than patient severity.

Program III-a. This Level III program, which shared the same hospital facilities and staff as Program II-a, provided detoxification and included mostly HMO patients. The HMO patients shared a similar degree of severity with a group of Level IV patients treated in the same area. However, the Level IV patients' insurance paid a higher reimbursement rate, encouraging assignment to Level IV care. Services offered for both the Level III and IV patients included a physical exam upon admission, monitoring of vital signs every shift change, daily individual counseling and treatment groups. Groups were conducted from 8:30 a.m. to 4:30 p.m. Patients had 2 hours of free time in the afternoons but remained on the unit. In the evening, patients attended a 12-step meeting and a wrap-up group.

Some tension was observed between medical and counseling staff. Counselors encouraged patients to address psychological issues around their addictions. Nurses emphasized patients' medical needs and felt the psychological approach might increase patient vulnerability without adequate time to work through important primary issues.

Duration of treatment varied by patient insurance and provider incentive. Patients in this Level III who were paid for by an HMO had their care reviewed daily and on-site HMO representatives encouraged step down to lower and less expensive LOCs as soon as possible. Patients with less intensively managed insurance benefits had longer lengths of stay within a level.

Program III-b. A publicly funded private non-profit residential women's treatment program, this Level III program was part of a larger organization. The program served 20 women with an average length of stay of 14 days. Fourteen counselors with college degrees and a full-time nurse staffed the unit, and a physician was available on call. Patients saw an individual counselor every other day. Each day, patients participated in 7 hours of group therapy guided by a manual provided by the parent organization. Groups included expressive therapy, substance abuse education, smoking cessation, and 12 step groups. Patients expressed appreciation for the attention they received. They liked the groups but wished they could have more individual counseling sessions.

Program III-c. Serving both men and women, this Level III program was primarily a detoxification unit, located in an old building on a public hospital campus. Unit space was cramped, and the facility was run-down. The summer heat in the building frequently shut down the research assistant's laptop computer and prompted patient and staff complaints. Because of the limited space, patients and staff also expressed privacy concerns. The atmosphere was characterized as depressing, the staff as solemn. Most patients had long-term histories of heroin addiction. The staff included a clinical director, a nursing supervisor, nursing staff and counselors, many of whom were in recovery. Staff tension was observed due to differences in staff training, heavy case loads, a recent patient death, and an infestation of cockroaches. Staff reported that they lacked sufficient time to both care for patients and complete patient assessments.

Program III-d. This Level III (non-acute) residential rehabilitation unit was located in an old Victorian house in need of repair. Although space was also cramped, the staff was cohesive, possibly because most shared similar training as counselors. Patients participated in a fully structured set of activities, from 6 a.m. until 10 p.m. There were 3 groups provided daily, plus an AA or NA meeting. Patients also were responsible for house maintenance chores. They made their own breakfast and lunch; dinner was provided.

Program III-e. This Level III detoxification unit was operated by a private non-profit organization that managed many other programs. According to staff, it served 35-40 patients and averaged 5 admissions a day. The census was 26 patients during the program assessment. Typical lengths of stay at this program were 7 days for detoxification from heroin and 5 days from alcohol and other drugs. The facility was located in a poor neighborhood with limited access to public transportation. Seventy percent of patients were homeless and 30 percent were dually diagnosed. The unit offered 3 skilled treatment services: group therapy, substance abuse education, HIV and health education; an AA or NA group also met on site. The staff included a physician who visited daily, counseling, nursing, and administrative staff. An emergency community outreach team could be called in during a crisis to do a psychiatric evaluation. There were 4 full-time counselors; most were non-degreed. It was observed that this program may have lacked sufficient nursing staff, and that all staff members were stressed by the intensity of their workload. The following observational data from this program illustrate some of the challenges and sources of variance within a level in managing patient severity and length of stay.

The program director, a nurse, indicated that the counseling staff encouraged homeless applicants who might otherwise qualify for Level II treatment to enter the Level III unit because homeless patients found it difficult to maintain sobriety while living in shelters. Thus, their level of severity may have been more similar to Level II patients than to other Level III patients.

Considerable tension was observed between nursing and counseling staff about the handling of high-risk patients. For example, counseling staff, some whom were in recovery, were comfortable working with one patient who was suicidal and one who was potentially violent. On the other hand, nursing staff felt they could not guarantee the safety of the suicidal patient, because no one was available to maintain close observation, or of the other patients and themselves because of the potentially violent patient.

Duration of treatment was another issue for staff. One way staff encouraged patients to stay in the detoxification program was to maintain them in hospital pajamas and robes. When patients sought to leave, they had to request their clothes and get dressed. This allowed counselors time to try to talk patients out of leaving against medical advice. Prior to the introduction of Medicaid managed care in the state, patients could reside in the detoxification unit for up to two weeks, but subsequently, staff indicated that they perceived that managed care, Medicaid, or state policy discouraged more than 5-7 days of treatment. With the shortened length of stay, staff felt they were unable to design and implement adequate discharge plans. The counseling staff was frustrated that they had so little time to place patients but the head counselor stated, "we have to remember our job is to safely detox people. Anything else we do is a plus."

1997 Site Visits

Five of the 9 original sites visited in 1995 remained in the study by 1997. Programs II-a and III-a, observed in 1995, were used as pilot sites to develop the observational study. Their information was included in Table 1 because of its interest. However, they did not participate in the ASAM Validity Study and were not revisited in 1997. Program II-c was awaiting a new contract from the state and was not operating in the fall of 1997. Program III-c was also not an ASAM Validity Study site but was included in Table 1 as a description of a detoxification site. Three new sites joined the ASAM Validity Study after 1995 and are described below. One is a Level II site, Program II-e, and 2 are Level III sites, Programs III-f and III-g. All of these sites were asked about the impact of managed care on the delivery of treatment. All programs said they provided treatment for clients with dual diagnoses of substance abuse and mental illness.

ASAM Level II Care Programs

Program II-b. This Level II site retained the same program it had in 1995. However, staff reported feeling constrained by shortened treatment time for the 85 percent of their clients whom, at this point, were insured through State managed care funds. One staff person said, "the current belief seems to be that within four days a long-term user can suddenly be clearer and make behavioral changes, which is unrealistic." Patients did not seem to be aware of any impact of managed care.

Program II-d. Two years later, this program had a larger group of clients, 8 observed most days, but the program remained of some concern. Four groups were offered each day, but one was an educational film and discussion and another an AA meeting. The program emphasized, in the words of one staff member, "sobriety in the moment . . . other areas of concern (e.g., school, work, and home life) are viewed as distractions and are not addressed." Furthermore, there was a tension between the need for flexibility to address client issues and the desire for structure that is thought to be crucial for this population. Managed care was not seen as affecting the delivery of treatment by staff or patients.

Program II-e. This program was similar to other Level II programs in that it operated about 5.5 hours each day and offered 3 groups during the day. Clients received a written treatment protocol and individualized programs. However, the program was relatively larger than the other Level II programs, with about 15 staff and 25 clients seen each day. About 60 percent of clients were publicly funded. Managed care was seen as having an effect on patient treatment, leading to "brief, solution focused therapy, shortened LOS, and behavioral outcome measures."

TABLE 1. ASAM programs observed in 1995

Level of Care	Level II Programs				Level III Programs				
Program #	*II-a*	*II-b*	*II-c*	*II-d*	*III-a*	*III-b*	*III-c*	*III-d*	*III-e*
Hours/day	8	5	6.5	5.5	24	24	24	24	24
Special Populations	no	women	50% dual dx	no	no	women	home-less	no	70% home-less
ALOS (days)	13	28	10	10-15	3-5	14	7	28	5-7 D 9 R
Direct access to Level	III, IV	I, III	I, III	IV	II, IV	II	I, II, III	I, II, III	I, II
Setting									
# Beds	-	-	-	-	16	20	47 D 8 S	20	50
# Pts/day	8-10	6-15	8-12	≤ 3	16	20	40	17	35-40
Nonprofit	yes	yes	yes	no	yes	yes	yes	yes	yes
% Publicly Financed Pts	< 50%	90%	75%	80%	10-20%	75%	95%	> 50%	90%
Staff									
Total	16	9	5	5	16	6	5	6	9
Total degreed*	11	9	5	5	11	4	3	2	3
Director's degree	MD	LICSW	MSN	MA	MD	BA	LICSW	LICSW	RN
Services									
Who does phys exam?	MD	none	RN avail	none	MD	none	MD	none	MD
1:1 therapy hrs/wk	2-3	1	2	1	2-3	3-5	1	1	1
Grp therapy hrs/day	4	4	5.5	3-4	5	7	3	3	5
Self-help/ Educ hrs/day	0	1	0	1	1	1	1	1	1
Dispense Rx	yes	yes	yes	no	yes	no	yes	no	yes

Tx = Treatment, D = Detox, R = Rehabilitation, S = Shelter; *Degreed: includes bachelors, RN, masters or doctoral.

One staff person suggested dissolving the state behavioral health carve-out so that substance abuse clients could receive more services.

ASAM Level III Care Programs

Program III-b. The structure of this program remained the same in 1997 as it was in 1995. The program was strict and highly structured, with clients beginning the day at 5:30 a.m. and scheduled activities that lasted until lights out at 11 p.m. Eighty-five percent of the clients had a dual diagnosis. Staff emphasized the need for greater integration of services for this population. They wished for more links with the state divisions of social service and mental health and for vocational rehabilitation services and transportation funds to get clients to appointments. Managed care affected only about 20 percent of their clients directly, but length of stay was shortened for these clients and limited their treatment.

Program III-d. This program also showed no evidence of change in its structure, but lengths of stay were shorter. A staff member said the "program has been streamlined to focus upon stabilization and referring for future treatment . . . [we] have gone from a 28 day program to a varying length of stay up to 25 days with average LOS of 10-14 days." The staff noted that many clients did not receive enough time in treatment, that no provision was made to allow time for exercise, and that salary levels were not high enough to hire clinicians trained to treat dually disordered clients.

Program III-e. This program continued to serve a complicated population with a high percentage of homeless men and women. The program offered individual treatment, groups, and case management services. The staff reported their program was well integrated with other community services, including a homeless outreach program, collaboration with a criminal justice program, affiliations with local medical centers and family health and social service agencies.

Program III-f. Located in the same building as a public hospital, the director of this program was a nurse with a RN degree. The program was highly structured and included several didactic educational groups along with groups that stressed role-playing and relaxation exercises. Most clients were publicly funded and the majority had managed care coverage. The program was designed to be 14 days, but the managed care organizations only allowed 10. The director routinely asked for more days for up to half of these clients. The staff felt that even 14 days was too short and that the program should be at least 21 days for everyone so that clients can absorb all the information offered to them. Another shortcoming pointed out by staff members was the lack of funds for prescriptions for some clients. Although clients could see physicians for health problems, many did not have the resources to pay for prescriptions.

Program III-g. This program also treated a complicated population, all of whom were publicly funded. Seventy percent were dually diagnosed. Managed care restricted length of stay for about 15 percent of the clients. Those clients received priority for case management and counseling services because they received fewer treatment days.

DISCUSSION

Do these treatment units meet ASAM level criteria? To a certain extent, they do. But there is tremendous variation around the parameters of a structured program, the correspondence between patients' clinical needs and services received, and the definition of skilled treatment services. Among the Level II programs observed, all had assigned treatment staff, 24-hour on-call emergency plans, an affiliation with another LOC, and offered an organized treatment regimen with at least group therapy as a skilled treatment service. Most also had individual therapy, although patients in all Level II units wanted more individual counseling than they received. Good staff cohesiveness was observed in Level II units, possibly because staff shared a similar counseling perspective.

However, patients' treatment experiences were very different, depending on the Level II program they attended. Staff training (masters level counselors vs. non-degreed counselors) and number and type of skilled treatment services tended to vary by program funding sources, or provider incentives. These factors were influential in whether programs provided more or less expensive treatment options. Distinctions between problems that were due to philosophical approaches (i.e., differences between staff disciplines) and those related to inadequate training could not be determined in this study but might be of interest in future research. Treatment services also varied by the type of affiliation. The Level II unit within a community hospital (Program II-a) could offer a wide range of services because those services were readily available in the adjacent Level III program (Program III-a). This same Level II program operated 8 hours a day; the other observed Level II units were open 5-6 hours a day. The women's program (Program II-b) was specifically designed to meet the needs of this special population, but clients were so diverse in Program II-d that a single group had to address very different patient needs. In some Level II programs, patients had daily individual therapy (Program II-a) while in others individual therapy occurred once a week (Program II-b).

As was true in Level II, all Level III units met basic ASAM LOC criteria: they had established beds, 24-hour treatment, and offered individual and group therapy. Three provided detoxification services (Programs III-a, III-c, and III-e). All had nursing and counseling staff. Tension occurred on these units over the different focus of treatment between nursing and counseling staff.

As observed among the Level II programs, there were notable differences among the Level III programs. Length of stay varied by funding source. Publicly funded facilities provided 14 days or more (Programs III-b and III-d) in rehabilitation programs, while privately insured HMO patients remained in Level III (Program III-a) just so long as their care manager observed their need for this LOC. Private pay patients in Program III-a received 2-3 hours of individual therapy a week, but public pay clients in Program III-c received individual therapy only 1 hour a week. Patients in Program III-b received 7 hours daily of group therapy while others (in Program III-d) participated in group therapy 3 hours a day. In Program III-b, counseling staff members provided group therapy following a manual-driven protocol. Other Level III programs provided group therapy, but it was more individualized and psychodynamic (e.g., Program III-d).

Managed care appears to be having an observable affect on the delivery of services in both Level II and Level III. It may be that the programming in Level II is becoming more fragmented as managed care organizations package treatment in hours or visits allowed, rather than in units of a treatment program. In Level III the impact of managed care seems to be increasingly ratcheting down length of stay while decreasing the integration of care between providers of substance abuse and mental health services. As residential programs have fewer days to treat people, less time can be spent on obtaining referrals for the time after treatment.

In conclusion, the checklist survey data provide good evidence that treatment in Level III is more intensive than that in Level II. Observational data corroborate the ASAM LOC descriptions as effectively distinguishing not only between settings, but also between program intensities, at least for the levels examined in this study. Level III acute rehabilitation in Massachusetts appears to have a focus on the medical needs of patients who are in detoxification or have recently been detoxified. There is a more structured treatment regimen with more individual therapy and more groups than patients receive in Level II. Field observation data also show the extent of the variation of services offered within LOCs.

It is likely that the same within-LOC variation found in these Massachusetts programs exists elsewhere to at least the same or possibly greater degree (given that Massachusetts had attempted to standardize LOC requirements through adoption of the ASAM Criteria). Another issue is that, already, the particular managed care era of this study has passed. The highly fluid current health care environment necessitates periodic re-evaluations of how closely programs meet LOC specifications, both for clinical purposes and for future research. Managed care has the potential to offer more people some time in care, but the risk is also present for reduced provider effectiveness. In the final analysis of the ASAM Criteria Validity Study and similar studies, it will be important to examine the effects of payment sources on treatment services offered within LOCs, and to take these variables into account when assessing patient outcomes. The crucial finding in this report is that standardized implementation of the ASAM Criteria warrants the development of formal methods for program evaluation with both quantitative and qualitative specifications. Further, without formal accounting of program specifications, the field risks multiple problems, including a destructive level of noise in research efforts, inability to determine safe and effective placement of patients in routine clinical practice, and ongoing conflicts between programs and managed care organizations struggling with unreliable program characterizations. These findings have important implications for program administrators, payers, and policymakers for the use of placement criteria in the real-world setting.

REFERENCES

1. Weisner C, McCarty D, Schmidt L. New directions in alcohol and drug treatment under managed care. American Journal of Managed Care. 1999;5:57-69.

2. Hoffmann NG, Halikas JA, Mee-Lee D, Weedman RD. Patient placement criteria for the treatment of psychoactive substance use disorders. Washington: American Society of Addiction Medicine, 1991.

3. Morey LC. Patient placement criteria: linking typologies to managed care. Alcohol Health & Research World. 1996;20:36-44.

4. Gastfriend DR, McLellan AT: Treatment matching: theoretic basis and practical implications. Med Clin N Amer. 1997;81:945-966.

5. Gastfriend DR, Lu SH, Sharon E. Placement matching: challenges and technical progress. Subst Use Misuse. 2000;35:2191-2213.

6. Gastfriend DR, Mee-Lee D. The ASAM patient placement criteria: context, concepts and continuing development. J Addict Dis. 2003; 22(Suppl. 1):1-8.

7. American Society of Addiction Medicine. Patient placement criteria for the treatment of substance-related disorders, second edition (ASAM PPC-2). Chevy Chase: American Society of Addiction Medicine, Inc., 1996.

8. Mee-Lee D, Shulman GD, Fishman M, et al., eds. ASAM patient placement criteria for the treatment of substance-related disorders, second edition-revised (ASAM PPC-2R). Chevy Chase: American Society of Addiction Medicine, Inc., 2001.

9. Levine HJ, Horgan C, Lee M, et al. The organization of the substance abuse treatment system: results from a national survey of facility directors. Schneider Institute for Health Policy, Heller Graduate School, Brandeis University, 2000.

10. Glaser N, Strauss A. The discovery of grounded theory. Chicago: Aldine Press, 1967.

11. Borkman TJ. Social-experiential model in programs for alcoholism: a research report on a new treatment design. Rockville: NIAAA, 1982.

12. Lyons M, Ziviani J. Stereotypes, stigma, and mental illness: learning from fieldwork experiences. Am J Occup Ther. 1995;49:1002-1008.

13. De Leon G, Inciardi JA, Martin SS. Residential drug abuse treatment research: are conventional control designs appropriate for assessing treatment effectiveness? J Psychoactive Drugs. 1995;27:85-91.

14. Heath DB. Quantitative and qualitative research on alcohol and drugs: a helpful reminder. Addiction. 1995;90:753-754.

15. McKeganey N. Quantitative and qualitative research in the addictions: an unhelpful divide. Addiction. 1995;90:749-751.

Impact of Patient Placement Criteria on Substance Abuse Treatment Under the Oregon Health Plan

Dennis Deck, PhD
Roy Gabriel, PhD
Jeff Knudsen, MA
Gwen Grams, PhD

SUMMARY. When Oregon shifted to managed care for Medicaid-funded substance abuse treatment, standardized patient placement and discharge criteria were rapidly implemented statewide.

This prospective, naturalistic study examines the validity and impact of placement criteria with a sample of 240 adults presenting for treatment compared to a sample of 287 in Washington state, where implementation was phased in slowly.

Dennis Deck, Roy Gabriel, and Jeff Knudsen are affiliated with the RMC Research Corporation, 522 SW Fifth Avenue, Suite 1407, Portland, OR 97204.

Gwen Grams is affiliated with the Office of Mental Health and Addiction Services, Oregon Department of Human Services, 500 Summer Street, NE E86, Salem, OR 97310-1016.

Address correspondence to: Dennis Deck, RMC Research Corporation, 522 SW Fifth Avenue, Suite 1407, Portland, OR 97204.

Supported in part by the Center for Substance Abuse Treatment, Substance Abuse and Mental Health Services Administration, Cooperative Agreement No. 1 UR7 TI 11294 01 and Grant No. 1KD1 TI12045-01.

[Haworth co-indexing entry note]: "Impact of Patient Placement Criteria on Substance Abuse Treatment Under the Oregon Health Plan." Deck, Dennis et al. Co-published simultaneously in *Journal of Addictive Diseases* (The Haworth Medical Press, an imprint of The Haworth Press, Inc.) Vol. 22, Supplement No. 1, 2003, pp. 27-44; and: *Addiction Treatment Matching: Research Foundations of the American Society of Addiction Medicine (ASAM) Criteria* (ed: David R. Gastfriend) The Haworth Medical Press, an imprint of The Haworth Press, Inc., 2003, pp. 27-44. Single or multiple copies of this article are available for a fee from The Haworth Document Delivery Service [1-800-HAWORTH, 9:00 a.m. - 5:00 p.m. (EST). E-mail address: docdelivery@haworthpress.com].

Digital Object Identifier: 10.1300/J069v22S01_03

Baseline profile analysis suggested better differentiation between Level II and Level III clients for the Oregon sample and better implementation than with the Washington sample, presumably because Oregon clinicians received more training and had more experience with the criteria. A majority of the Oregon sample was placed in intensive outpatient programs, consistent with the recommended level of care.

In this study, placement criteria showed good potential for changing treatment planning behavior, increasing individualization, and improving utilization of new levels of care. *[Article copies available for a fee from The Haworth Document Delivery Service: 1-800-HAWORTH. E-mail address: <docdelivery@haworthpress.com> Website: <http://www.HaworthPress.com>*

KEYWORDS. ASAM levels of care, treatment matching criteria, substance abuse

BACKGROUND

During the past 10 years considerable research attention has been given to the multifaceted needs of clients presenting for substance abuse treatment and the level of care needed to ensure maximal outcomes for all types of clients. At the same time, the rapid growth of managed behavioral health care created an urgent need for standards or criteria that can guide client placement. This paper examines the impact of implementing standardized placement and discharge criteria in Oregon as part of an effort to integrate public sector substance abuse treatment with physical health care while protecting against the problems experienced in other states.

Patient Placement Criteria

The development of methods to match patients selectively to optimal levels of care can be traced to two concurrent shifts in the structure of substance abuse treatment. First, it has become increasingly apparent over the last decade that the heterogeneity of the chemically dependent population requires a diversity of both treatment modalities and levels of care.[1,2] Second, and somewhat unexpectedly, the proliferation of managed care systems has begun to require specific modalities and levels of care to control and contain costs.[3,4] Increasing concern that treatment placement decisions will be based on financial consideration rather than client needs (e.g., that managed care might eliminate higher, more expensive levels of care) has prompted treatment providers and state officials to adopt criteria to ensure valid and cost-effective treatment matching for treatment modalities and levels of care.

In an effort to provide nonproprietary placement criteria, the National Association of Addiction Treatment Providers and the American Society of Addiction Medicine (ASAM) collaborated to produce the first edition of the ASAM patient placement criteria.[5] Ongoing concerns over the cost-effectiveness of the 1991 criteria led to the development of a new coalition that included representatives from managed care organizations, government agencies involved in statewide Medicaid programs, researchers, and providers.[2] The end product of this collaborative effort, ASAM's 1996 *Patient Placement Criteria for the Treatment of Substance-Related Disorders, Second Edition* (PPC-2)[6] is still in effect today, although a revision, the PPC-2R, was published in 2001.

The PPC-2 maintained the 6 patient dimensions and the 4 levels of care from the first edition but incorporated several critical changes. One of these changes involved the addition of subclassifications to the 4 levels and the inclusion of a new level of care called *early intervention*. Other broader, paradigmatic changes to the second edition included a shift from unidimensional to multidimensional assessment, program-driven to clinically driven treatment, fixed length of service to variable length of service, and a limited number of discrete levels of care to a continuum of care (see Gastfriend & Mee-Lee, elsewhere in this issue).[6]

DEVELOPMENT OF OREGON'S PATIENT PLACEMENT CRITERIA

Driven by concern over the rising cost of medical care and the growing number of people remaining uninsured, the Oregon legislature passed a series of laws from 1989 through 1993 known collectively as the Oregon Health Plan (OHP).[7,8] The state's well-documented *rationing* process began with a rank ordering of 696 medical *condition/treatment pairs*, in terms of their clinical effectiveness and value to society, for coverage under OHP. Initially, 565 of these pairs were included in OHP coverage, with chemical dependency ranked 182nd on the list. When Oregon was granted a 5-year, federal Medicaid waiver by the Health Care Financing Administration in 1994, the state expanded Medicaid eligibility to include all adults and their dependents whose income was below the federal poverty limit, which more than doubled the size of the eligible population to 13% of Oregon's population. Mandatory enrollment in 1 of 19 prepaid health plans was phased in over the next year, thus shifting responsibility of Medicaid-financed health services to managed care.

In May 1995, Oregon integrated the chemical dependency benefit (including outpatient treatment, intensive outpatient treatment, methadone services, and limited hospital-based detoxification treatment) into OHP. Thus Oregon became one of the first states to implement capitated financing for Medicaid alcohol and drug treatment services. Increased referrals to treatment from primary care physicians and reduced long-term health costs were two of the expected outcomes of an integrated chemical dependency benefit. Yet concerns persisted that access to care or utilization of services might be reduced under managed care, and state officials also built in several safeguards.

In an effort to develop a common framework for the managed care organizations and to eliminate concerns that placement decisions would be based on financial rather than clinical considerations, Oregon's Office of Alcohol and Drug Abuse Programs (OADAP) worked with key stakeholders over a 2-year period to develop client placement and discharge criteria.[9,10] Oregon aimed to develop criteria that (a) are as objective, measurable, and quantifiable as possible; (b) place the patient at the least intensive treatment level without sacrificing treatment objectives or patient safety and security; (c) provide a continuum of care; and (d) avoid treatment failure. Using the first edition of ASAM placement criteria as a starting point, the working group made some language modifications to make Oregon's placement criteria more accessible to the treatment community. The resulting guidelines, sometimes referred to as "OSAM," remained, however, very similar to the original ASAM criteria in most respects. Although problems stemming from the implementation of a new system were inevitable,[11] the state agency offered numerous training sessions that, at minimum, introduced providers to the placement criteria.

The new Oregon Administrative Rule (OAR 415-51-030) pertinent to these changes stipulated that the treatment protocol could vary from agency to agency, but providers should develop treatment plans, progress notes, and discharge plans consistent with Oregon's placement criteria for all outpatient and intensive outpatient treatment (but excluding residential treatment).

METHODS

As part of a larger study of the impact of managed care on the utilization and outcomes of substance abuse treatment services under OHP,[12-14] we collected data that reflect the implementation of patient placement criteria. This study included 4 components: interviews with a prospective sample of clients beginning a new treatment episode, a chart review of provider records, analyses of population-level administrative data describing the utilization of treatment services, and a qualitative study of stakeholder experiences and perceptions of substance abuse treatment under managed care.

The design of these studies included recruiting a comparison group from the demographically similar, neighboring state of Washington. Community providers are responsible for substance abuse treatment services in both states; and both state systems include limitations on the duration and intensity of services provided in various treatment modalities. In both states, the Medicaid benefit covers outpatient and methadone services but other sources are used to fund residential and detoxification services. However, Washington clients have greater access to residential services and the state funds a special program for indigent substance users.

Unlike Oregon, Washington does not contract with managed care organizations for the organization and financing of its Medicaid substance abuse treatment services. The state agency that manages substance abuse treatment programs in Washington, the Division of Alcohol and Substance Abuse within the Department of Social and Health Services, recognized the value of standardized placement criteria and adopted the ASAM placement criteria. However, they did not provide the level of training and support described in Oregon, and they did not require implementation of these criteria until 1997, more than 2 years after Oregon mandated the use of its placement criteria.

Prospective Study

The prospective study included structured interviews with clients entering a new treatment episode and client chart reviews. The interviews employed a standardized interview protocol administered at treatment episode entry (baseline) and again at 6 months and 12 months following the initial interview.

The interview protocol consisted of 9 domains of information and was adapted from several standardized instruments frequently used in the substance abuse research literature including the Addiction Severity Index,[15] the SF-12,[16] the Brief Symptom Inventory,[17] and the Risk for AIDS Behavior scale.[18] The subscales used in the prospective study measured physical health status and use of health care services, alcohol and other drug use, mental health symptoms, involvement in the criminal justice system, employment and financial support, and sexual behavior and risk of AIDS.

Completion of baseline interviews resulted in a sample of 240 clients recruited from providers under contract with Regence HMO Oregon, the largest prepaid plan, and 287 clients recruited from Washington. Recruitment in Washington was restricted to counties that were similar in demographics and other characteristics to the Oregon counties served by Regence HMO Oregon. The study team monitored client characteristics throughout the recruitment period to ensure the equivalence of the 2 samples. Analysis of baseline data confirmed that the 2 state samples were largely equivalent in terms of demographics, substance use history, and service use.[12,19] Table 1 displays the similarity in demographic characteristics of the two samples for clients included in the comparative analyses presented here. The Washington sample appears somewhat more ethnically diverse than Oregon's, but this is consistent with differences in the states' general populations. The Washington sample also reports less social support and less residential stability. Using the Bonferonni method to control the Type I error rate across comparisons, however, only the difference in marital status is statistically significant.

Table 2 summarizes the mean differences between the groups on each of the baseline scales. A MANOVA confirmed that there were state differences ($F = 4.67$, $p < .001$, $df = 4, 484$) across the 10 scales. The Oregon sample reported greater alcohol use and physical health limitations while the Washington sample reported greater legal and employment problems.

These results reveal some qualitative group differences in client characteristics and severity of symptoms. However, these differences do not suggest an overall difference in severity favoring either state that would explain differences in client placement or discharge.

Chart Review

The intent of the provider chart review was to describe each client's utilization of treatment services and to triangulate these data with service utilization data collected by self-report and state data systems. The study team developed a standard protocol to guide abstraction of the provider records to determine client placement level, treatment modality, wraparound services, and type and intensity of treatment services received. Senior members of the study team solicited cooperation from the executive director of each treatment agency.

TABLE 1. Client characteristics in Oregon and Washington samples.

	Percent of Clients	
Characteristic	Oregon (N = 208)	Washington (N = 265)
Female	56	58
Racial/ethnic group*		
• White (not Hispanic)	81	73
• Black (not Hispanic)	7	17
• Hispanic	5	6
• Other	6	4
Age		
• 18-30	35	35
• 31-45	55	56
• 46-64	10	9
Mandated to treatment	26	24
Marital status*		
• Married	17	9
• Living as married	27	13
• Widowed/divorced/separated	31	35
• Never married	26	43
Homeless in past 6 months	23	33
IV drug use in past 6 months	20	23

*$p < .01$

Trained data collectors conducted a review of treatment provider records on each client at 6 months following intake to treatment. Chart reviews were completed for 208 clients in Oregon and 265 clients in Washington, equal to 94% of the baseline interview sample. Charts were unavailable for 32 clients, usually because the records had been archived before the data collector visited the site.

Qualitative Study

The qualitative study sought to determine the impact of the transition to managed care on treatment providers and to describe providers' ex-

TABLE 2. Mean severity at entry to treatment on 10 scales for Oregon and Washington samples.

Baseline Severity Measure	Oregon (N = 208)		Washington (N = 263)	
	M	*SD*	*M*	*SD*
ASI alcohol composite*	.172	.260	.123	.203
ASI drug composite	.096	.122	.087	.112
RAB HIV drug risk scale	.056	.149	.087	.206
ASI psychiatric composite	.274	.272	.235	.245
SF-12 mental health	39.6	14.2	39.3	13.9
BSI depression scale	.942	.900	.965	.910
ASI medical composite	.340	.370	.323	.369
SF-12 physical health*	46.1	11.3	48.6	10.5
ASI employment composite*	.732	.284	.829	.233
ASI legal composite*	.124	.194	.176	.216

*$p < .05$

periences working within a managed care system. Study staff conducted interviews with 18 clinical directors and other staff drawn from a purposive sample of the 20 treatment agencies under contract to Regence HMO Oregon. A second wave of interviews that included state officials and managed care representatives clarified and expanded upon themes uncovered in the analysis of the initial interviews. All interviews were recorded, transcribed, coded, and entered into the AnSWR[20] qualitative data analysis program. An analyst identified themes using an inductive analysis process[21] that involved iterative reduction, convergence, and coding.

RESULTS

The analysis compared the clinically derived levels with actual placements in treatment modalities and with the severity measures embedded in client interviews. The relationship between assigned levels and treatment intensity and duration was also assessed.

Treatment Modality

Figure 1 shows that the pattern of treatment modality into which clients in the 2 samples were placed differs considerably ($\chi^2 = 21.8$, $df = 4$, $p < .001$). Although slight differences for residential drug-free and methadone maintenance treatment were evident, the important differences were in regular and intensive outpatient treatment. Three-fifths (60%) of the Oregon sample was placed in intensive outpatient compared to two-fifths (41%) of the Washington sample. Conversely, one-third (33%) of the Oregon sample was placed in regular outpatient compared to nearly half (45%) of the Washington sample.

Correspondence to Placement Level

Table 3 compares the actual placement of clients with the ASAM level assigned by a clinician. Overall, there was 95% agreement (174 out of 183) between the actual placement in treatment and the clinical recommendation in the Oregon sample and 81% (140 out of 172) in the Washington sample. In Oregon, 5 out of 14 Level III clients had been placed in intensive outpatient settings rather than drug-free residential programs. Further investigation revealed that these 5 clients had just

FIGURE 1. Distribution of treatment modality for Orgeon and Washington samples.

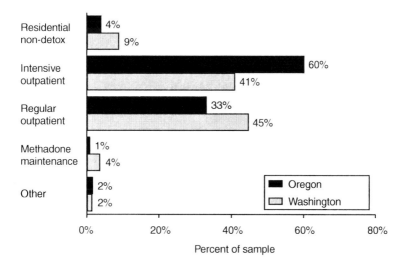

TABLE 3. Comparison of treatment modality with clinical recommendation (ASAM level of care) for Oregon and Washington samples.

| | Oregon | | | | Washington | | | | |
| | Level | | | | Level | | | | |
Treatment Modality	I	II	III	IV	.5	I	II	III	IV
Residential drug-free	0	0	9	0					
Intensive outpatient	3	101	5	1	1	7	68	1	0
Regular outpatient	64	0	0	0	7	72	7	8	1

Note. Blank cells = not applicable.

been transferred from a short-term residential setting as they began their index treatment episode for inclusion in this study. In Washington 15 clients with Level II or III recommendations were placed in regular outpatient programs and 8 clients with an early intervention (.5) recommendation were placed in outpatient or intensive outpatient programs. Clinical recommendations were unavailable for 10 Washington clients in residential programs and 7 methadone placements were excluded from the table.

Validation of Placement Level

Figure 2 illustrates the relationship between the level of care recommended by the clinician through the application of the placement criteria and an independent assessment of severity obtained from the baseline interview. Each line represents the self-reported severity profile for clients assessed at one level of care. For these profiles, scores are expressed as standardized Z-scores ($M = 0$, $SD = 1$) to place each of the 10 outcome measures on the same scale. A higher mean reflects greater severity in that domain.

For Oregon, we observed a difference of approximately 0.5 standard deviation between Level II and Level III clients on many of the scales, whereas a modest difference of about 0.2 standard deviation was observed between Level I and Level II clients on only a few scales. We conducted a profile analysis[22] by testing for parallelism (an interaction) before testing level differences. A MANOVA conducted on the slopes (differences between adjacent measures) was not significant ($F = .84$, ns, $df = 18, 368$), but a MANOVA conducted on the levels was significant ($F = 2.02, p < .01, df = 20, 366$). The univariate F-tests revealed that

FIGURE 2. Average Z-scores ($M = 0$, $SD = 1$) on 10 self-reported severity scales for Oregon and Washington clients clinically evaluated at 3 levels of care at intake to treatment. The number of cases were 74, 107, and 14 for Oregon; 80, 79, and 10 for Washington.

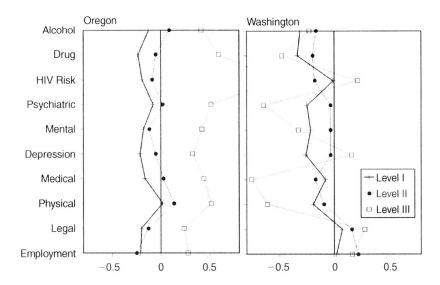

only the Addiction Severity Index drug composite ($F = 3.31$, $df = 2$, $p < .05$) and the Risk for Aids Behavior Drug scale reached statistical significance ($F = 14.8$, $df = 2$, $p < .001$). Unfortunately, the small number of Level III clients and the substantial within-level variance limit the statistical power of this analysis. A MANOVA conducted on only the Level I and Level II clients was not significant ($F = .61$, ns, $df = 10, 170$).

The Washington profile was somewhat different, and no monotonic relationship between the severity levels was evident. The Level III profile was particularly erratic, even for scales that measure related constructs (e.g., Addiction Severity Index psychiatric composite, SF-12 mental health scale, and Brief Symptom Inventory depression scale), but interpretation of this profile must be tempered by the small sample. Neither the test for parallelism ($F = .84$, ns, $df = 18, 368$) nor the levels test was significant ($F = 1.45$, ns, $df = 20, 314$).

Intensity of Treatment

To examine the relationship between placement and service intensity, Table 4 gives the average hours per week of individual and group

TABLE 4. Average therapy hours per week by modality.

Placement	Oregon			Washington		
	M	SD	n	M	SD	n
Regular outpatient	1.43	1.05	68	2.10	1.17	119
Intensive outpatient	3.55	2.43	131	3.60	2.18	110

therapy received by clients in regular outpatient and intensive outpatient modalities. For both states, adults in intensive outpatient settings received a greater intensity of services on average than clients in regular outpatient settings ($F = 92.4$, $df = 2$, $p < .001$), though considerable variation occurred within the groups due to poor attendance by many clients in both settings.

Length of Stay

To examine the impact of the discharge criteria, Figure 3 plots the length of stay for clients in each sample who completed treatment during the 180-day observation period. Clients who withdrew from treatment were excluded from the analysis because the application of discharge criteria did not impact their length of stay. The pattern for Oregon reveals considerable variability in length of stay with over half discharged after more than 90 days. The pattern for Washington shows that over half the discharges occurred at 90 days, the target duration for clients served under the state's Alcoholism and Drug Addiction Treatment and Support Act (ADATSA) program.[23] Levene's test for equality of variance confirmed that the length of stay for the Oregon sample was more variable ($F = 5.45$, $p < .05$) though the mean lengths of stay did not differ.

DISCUSSION

Oregon's implementation of client placement and discharge criteria under OHP offered a unique opportunity to examine the impact of such criteria on a publicly funded substance abuse treatment system. Although the original intent of implementing placement criteria was to control the influence of managed care on placement decisions, interviews with treatment providers clearly indicated that implementing the

FIGURE 3. Distribution of length of stay for clients completing treatment.

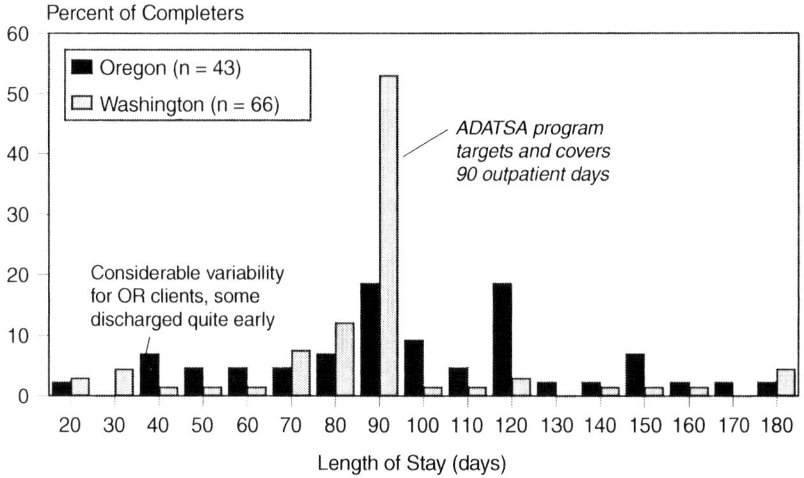

placement criteria also had a profound impact on provider behavior and the experience of transitioning to a managed care service delivery model. Providers generally reported that implementing placement criteria promoted greater professionalism and accountability among drug counselors, leading to more appropriate placements. The use of placement and discharge criteria led to a patient-driven rather than program-driven focus. The criteria have created a common language that has facilitated communication among providers, insurers, and state officials.

Providers also suggested, however, that the placement criteria have contributed to a universal paperwork burden. Clinicians reportedly struggled with the language or application of the criteria. Furthermore, Oregon providers maintained that the relative scarcity of residential treatment (a modality not covered in the Medicaid benefit but supported with state block grant funds) and limited coverage of inpatient services posed a dilemma in applying the criteria because the most appropriate placements for Level III and IV clients were often unavailable.

Intensity of Outpatient Services

The high utilization of intensive outpatient services in the Oregon sample led us to suspect that the implementation of placement criteria

drew the attention of providers to the idea that some clients would benefit from greater intensity outpatient services. Little evidence exists to
suggest that providers gave much attention to levels of care within the
outpatient treatment modality prior to implementation of the standardized placement criteria, though individual providers might have routinely customized the intensity of treatment plans.

This notion is consistent with the overriding themes in provider interviews though the respondents did not frame their observations in this
way. Providers acknowledged the impact of placement criteria on practice, but few specifically mentioned greater intensity of outpatient services as a consequence of the implementation of the placement criteria.
Although these results suggest an important impact of client placement
criteria, we must try to rule out alternative explanations.

Other differences between the states could have played a role in the
concentration in intensive outpatient services, such as a greater need for
more intensive treatment in the Oregon sample. Random assignment to
conditions was impossible, but the study team attempted to recruit
equivalent samples from a substantial cross-section of providers in each
state. The comparison of client characteristics and baseline scales for
these samples revealed some differences but did not suggest any consistent difference in severity favoring either state. The general lack of social supports among the Washington sample would justify a greater
intensity of care as well as the greater severity of alcohol use among the
Oregon sample. Of course, preexisting differences between the groups
on dimensions not included in our baseline interview battery might also
have been a factor.

To ensure that the increase in the intensity of outpatient treatment
services was not restricted to one prepaid plan, we conducted a population-level analysis of Medicaid claims and encounter data. Among
Medicaid claims for substance abuse treatment services provided in
1993, the average monthly intensity of individual and group therapy in
outpatient settings was 6.75 hours a month (about 1.69 hours per week).
In encounter records for treatment services provided during 1997, the
average outpatient intensity for clients enrolled in prepaid plans was
8.22 per month (about 2.05 hour per week), a 22% increase in the average intensity of therapy. Thus the implementation of client placement
criteria was associated with an overall increase in the intensity of outpatient therapy. Although we cannot eliminate the possibility of other
causal factors, the most plausible explanation is that more clients had a
treatment plan that specified a higher intensity of services as providers
gained experience with the placement criteria.

In one of the few studies of intensive outpatient programs, McLellan et al.[24] argued that greater intensity of core services is necessary but not sufficient to produce broader rehabilitative gains. We saw little evidence that Level II clients in either state received more support services.

Individualization

One theme prominent in the provider interviews was that implementing placement and discharge criteria promoted greater individualization in client care. The general perception was that proper use of the criteria leads to a more individualized length of stay and more appropriate assessment and placement. That is, treatment decisions would be based on client needs rather than the services an agency can offer or the number of arrests for driving under the influence of alcohol a client has. Providers also noted that clinicians' skills improved through use of the placement criteria because the criteria require holistic assessment and the regular consideration of different treatment modalities across the 6 dimensions.

The analysis of the length of stay for early treatment completers provides some empirical support for these perspectives. Clients who completed treatment within 180 days of intake into treatment in Oregon showed greater variability in length of stay compared to their Washington counterparts. This variability was consistent with the assertion that Oregon clients were discharged early on the basis of their progress. The provider interviews suggest that the application of discharge criteria played an important role in discharge decisions. The early discharges in Washington, in contrast, appear to have been driven more often by the limited funding available for a portion of the clients in this sample. Unfortunately, because nearly half of the clients in both states were still enrolled in treatment when the chart review was conducted, examining the duration of treatment over the full episode of care was not possible.

Validity of Placement

The severity scales embedded in the baseline interviews provided an independent means of validating the clinically derived client placement levels. The severity profiles by client placement level suggest that placement criteria were better implemented for the Oregon sample. Whereas the Oregon profile appeared consistent with expectations, the Washington profile evidenced less differentiation between levels and erratic results for the small Level III sample. Discussions with officials and providers in both states confirmed this interpretation. The conclusion was that Oregon providers had many more training opportunities and a shorter timeline for implementing placement criteria. These data were collected after statewide implementation in Oregon but before the deadline for implementation in Washington had passed. Our own observations suggest that the implementation deadline was the critical motivating factor.

The general lack of differences on the severity scales among the recommended levels of care does, however, raise the question of the reliability and validity of even those client placement decisions made by clinicians with fairly extensive training. Considerable variability within each level on each severity scale was evident. Despite the generally positive reaction to the criteria among the treatment providers we interviewed, respondents raised significant concerns about the application of placement criteria that deserve attention. For example, clinicians reported that the training was insufficient, the language of the criteria was unfamiliar or confusing, and the criteria were very subjective.

In-depth interviews with providers revealed varying impressions of the reliability and validity of the placement criteria. Some providers reported that Oregon's criteria are clearly stated and objective and yield accountability, accurate record keeping, and more consistent placement decisions. Other respondents expressed a concern that the criteria cannot take into account the myriad exigencies of a client's life that may make a particular type of treatment advantageous or prohibitive, underscoring the importance of allowing the experiential and subjective knowledge of the clinician to play a pivotal role in the final recommendation. Still others suggested that the placement criteria can be easily manipulated and have only changed the way clinicians write up assessments, not how they make assessments.

Turner et al.[25] noted that the complexity of the 1991 ASAM criteria raises serious questions about whether acceptable standards of reliability are attainable by the average clinician. Future studies should incorporate instruments that better reflect the clinical thinking about client needs embodied in the ASAM placement criteria. For example, the *Global Appraisal of Individual Need*[26] includes scales that explicitly attempt to assess each of the ASAM dimensions, and the instrument has been used extensively with outpatient populations similar to those entering the community substance abuse treatment system. Certainly, further work to establish the reliability and validity of placement criteria is needed.

REFERENCES

1. Project MATCH Research Group. Project MATCH (Matching Alcoholism Treatment to Client Heterogeneity): rationale and methods for a multisite clinical trial matching patients to alcoholism treatment. Alcohol Clin Exp Res. 1993;17:1130-1145.

2. Gastfriend DR, McLellan AT. Treatment matching: theoretical basis and practical implications. Alcohol and Other Substance Abuse. 1997;81:945-965.

3. Morey LC. Patient placement criteria: linking typologies to managed care. Alcohol Health Res World. 1996;20:36-44.

4. Galanter M, Keller DS, Dermatis H, Egelko S. The impact of managed care on addiction treatment: a problem in need of solution. Washington DC: American Society of Addiction Medicine; 1999. Available at: <http://www.asam.org/ppol/managedcare.htm>.

5. Hoffman N, Halikas J, Mee-Lee D, Weedman RD. ASAM-Patient Placement Criteria for the treatment of psychoactive substance use disorders. Washington DC: American Society of Addiction Medicine; 1991.

6. American Society of Addiction Medicine. Patient Placement Criteria for the treatment of substance-related disorders: second edition (ASAM PPC-2). Chevy Chase, MD; 1996.

7. Penner NR, McFarland BH. Background on the Oregon Health Plan. In: Goetz RR, McFarland BH, Ross KV, eds: What the Oregon Health Plan can teach us about managed mental health care. San Francisco: Jossey-Bass; 2000.

8. Gold M. Markets and public programs: insights from Oregon and Tennessee. J Health Polit. 1997;22,631-666.

9. Office of Alcohol and Drug Abuse Programs. Chemical dependency placement, continued stay and discharge criteria: adult. Salem, OR: Office of Alcohol and Drug Abuse Programs; 1995.

10. Office of Alcohol and Substance Abuse Programs. Chemical dependency placement, continued stay and discharge criteria: adolescent. Salem, OR: Office of Alcohol and Substance Abuse Programs; 1995.

11. Mondeaux FP, D'Ambrosio R. Publicly funded chemical dependency treatment in Oregon: transition from a fee-for-service to a managed care system. Paper presented at: Annual Meeting of the American Evaluation Association; 1999; Orlando, FL.

12. Gabriel R, Deck D, Mondeaux F, Brown K. The impact of managed care on chemical dependency treatment: three years under the Oregon Health Plan. Paper presented at: Annual Meeting of the American Public Health Association; 1998; Washington, DC.

13. Brown K, Gabriel RM. Six-month outcomes of treatment: managed care vs. nonmanaged care clients in Oregon and Washington. Paper presented at: Annual Meeting of the Association for Health Services Research; 1999; Chicago, IL.

14. Deck DD, McFarland BH, Titus JM, Laws KE, et al. Access to substance abuse treatment under the Oregon Health Plan. JAMA. 2000;284:2093-2099.

15. McLellan AT, Cacciola J, Kushner H, Peters R, et al. The fifth edition of the Addiction Severity Index: cautions, additions and normative data. J Subst Abuse Treatment. 1992; 9:461-480.

16. Ware JE, Sherbourne CD. The MOS 36-Item Short-Form Health Status Survey (SF-36): Part I conceptual framework and item selection. Med Care. 1992;30:253-265.

17. Derogatis LR, Melisaratos N. The Brief Symptom Inventory: an introductory report. Psychol Med. 1983;13:596-605.

18. Mesker D. Risk Assessment Battery (RAB). Pennsylvania, PA: University of Pennsylvania & Veterans Administration Medical Center, Center for Studies on Addiction; 1992.

19. Deck D, Gabriel R. Characteristics of adults entering publicly-funded chemical dependency treatment: challenges for assessing treatment outcomes. Paper presented at: Annual Meeting of the American Evaluation Association; 1998; Chicago, IL.

20. Centers for Disease Control and Prevention. Analysis software for word-based records (AnSWR; Version 2.0) [Software]. Atlanta, GA: Centers for Disease Control and Prevention; 1999.

21. Patton MQ. Qualitative evaluation and research methods (2nd ed). Newbury, Park, CA: Sage; 1990.

22. Harris RJ. A primer of multivariate statistics. New York: Academic Press; 1975.

23. Longhi D, Oatis S, Mudar K, Spaeth D, et al. The ADATSA program: clients, services, and treatment outcomes. Olympia, WA: Washington State Department of Social and Health Services, Office of Research and Data Analysis; 1991. Report No. 4-17.

24. McLellan AT, Hagan TA, Meyers K, Randall M, et al. "Intensive" outpatient substance abuse treatment: comparisons with "traditional" outpatient treatment. J Addictive Diseases. 1997;16:57-84.

25. Turner WM, Turner KH, Reif S, Gutowski WE, et al. Feasibility of multidimensional substance abuse treatment matching: automating the ASAM patient placement criteria. Drug and Alcohol Depend. 1999;55:35-43.

26. Dennis ML. Global Appraisal of Individual Needs: administration guide for the GAIN and related measures (Version 1299). Bloomington, IL: Chestnut Health Systems; 1999. Available at: <www.chestnut.org/li/gain>.

Reliability of Multidimensional Substance Abuse Treatment Matching: Implementing the ASAM Patient Placement Criteria

Sharon L. Baker, PhD
David R. Gastfriend, MD

SUMMARY. For meaningful adoption, the Patient Placement Criteria (PPC) of the American Society of Addiction Medicine (ASAM) will need adequate interrater reliability. In a decision analysis of the original PPC, we reduced potential sources of unreliability, mapped question items from clinical research instruments to each decision point, and programmed the item map as a computerized structured interview. Then, target videotapes from eight substance dependent adults who had been distributed by the algorithm into three levels of care (LOC) were independently scored by four raters who were blind as to ASAM LOC. The

Sharon L. Baker and David R. Gastfriend are affiliated with the Addiction Research Program, Department of Psychiatry, Massachusetts General Hospital and Harvard Medical School.

Address correspondence to: David R. Gastfriend, MD, Director, Addiction Research Program, Massachusetts General Hospital, 388 Commonwealth Avenue, Lower Level, Boston, MA 02115 (E-mail: DGastfriend@Partners.org).

Supported by Grants # R01-DA08781 and K24-DA00427 from the National Institute on Drug Abuse.

[Haworth co-indexing entry note]: "Reliability of Multidimensional Substance Abuse Treatment Matching: Implementing the ASAM Patient Placement Criteria." Baker, Sharon L., and David R. Gastfriend. Co-published simultaneously in *Journal of Addictive Diseases* (The Haworth Medical Press, an imprint of The Haworth Press, Inc.) Vol. 22, Supplement No. 1, 2003, pp. 45-60; and: *Addiction Treatment Matching: Research Foundations of the American Society of Addiction Medicine (ASAM) Criteria* (ed: David R. Gastfriend) The Haworth Medical Press, an imprint of The Haworth Press, Inc., 2003, pp. 45-60. Single or multiple copies of this article are available for a fee from The Haworth Document Delivery Service [1-800-HAWORTH, 9:00 a.m. - 5:00 p.m. (EST). E-mail address: docdelivery@haworthpress.com].

Digital Object Identifier: 10.1300/J069v22S01_04

45

intraclass correlation coefficient for ASAM LOC assignment was .77. For all but two subscales of component instruments, values were above .70 and significant, indicating high interrater reliability. With these methods, excellent reliability is possible for complex decision trees, making it possible to improve the validity of the ASAM Criteria and similar complex hierarchical clinical protocols. *[Article copies available for a fee from The Haworth Document Delivery Service: 1-800-HAWORTH. E-mail address: <docdelivery@haworthpress.com> Website: <http://www.HaworthPress. com> © 2003 by The Haworth Press, Inc. All rights reserved.]*

KEYWORDS. ASAM assessment, structured interview, inter-rater reliability, substance abuse assessment

BACKGROUND

Chronic diseases, particularly psychiatric disorders and psychoactive substance use disorders, have multifactorial etiologies and diverse manifestations, such that outcome prediction and treatment planning require multidimensional assessment. Despite growing empirical support for the idea of modality matching and placement matching in substance abuse treatment, the task of matching specific patients to specific treatments has proven to be complex and elusive.[1,2] Treatment matching was studied in two large multi-center trials, Project MATCH[2] and the U.S. Veterans Administration's Program Evaluation and Research Center,[3] with little support for matching patients to single-model behavioral therapies. Placement matching differs in two ways: it seeks to match patients to settings in which multiple treatment modalities may be combined, and it utilizes a medical perspective in addition to the psychosocial. Although empirical support for placement matching is still under investigation, integrating medical and psychosocial variables potentially offers greater breadth for successful matching.

The original Patient Placement Criteria (PPC-1) of the American Society of Addiction Medicine (ASAM)[4] and its revised editions[5,6] represent the most significant development to date in the process of establishing a single, standardized set of criteria for matching substance-abusing patients to the most appropriate setting.[1,7,8] This complex, hierarchical decision tree matches patients on the basis of the intensity of treatment required, referred to as levels of care (LOC). Four LOCs were initially defined: Level I–outpatient treatment, Level II–intensive outpatient treatment, Level III–medically monitored inpatient treatment and Level IV–medically managed inpatient treatment.[4] The ASAM Criteria have achieved widespread adoption, with their use recommended by over 20 states, by the U.S. Veterans Administration hospitals, and by the U.S. Department of Defense worldwide for its military personnel and dependents. While the ASAM Criteria approach has face validity, it has yet to be empirically validated in field trials.[9] Establishing the validity of decisions derived from the PPC in relation to clinical outcome measures is a critical step in any consideration of their widespread implementation in treatment matching.[10]

The question of the validity of the ASAM PPC cannot be considered independently of the question of reliability. Whereas validity refers to whether an instrument actually measures what it purports to measure, reliability refers to the consistency of that measurement. It is commonly understood in psychometric research that the reliability of a given measure determines the upper limit of its validity, i.e., one cannot have an instrument that is more valid than it is reliable. To paraphrase Del Boca et al.,[11] reliable measurement of the ASAM PPC represents a necessary though not sufficient condition for establishing their validity. Consequently, in order to demonstrate that the PPC has validity, it must be implemented in such a way that assignment to LOC is based on a set of information that is consistently obtained and systematically applied to the decision rules.

A multi-site study conducted through the Massachusetts General Hospital (MGH) sought to establish the validity of these criteria for the two middle LOCs, i.e., day treatment (Level II) and non-hospital inpatient treatment (Level III), using a match-mismatch design. This study was conducted in collaboration with the Massachusetts Department of Public Health Bureau of Substance Abuse Services, the Massachusetts Department of Medical Assistance, and the Massachusetts Behavioral Health Partnership. This ASAM Criteria Validity Study recruited substance dependent subjects from substance abuse treatment intake sites, assessed them for the LOC recommended by the first edition of the ASAM Criteria, randomly matched or mismatched the subjects to either a day treatment or a non-hospital inpatient setting and then followed the subjects for one year to determine if any treatment outcome advantages resulted for the matched vs. mismatched groups.

The PPC relies upon a dimensional approach to assessment which takes into account a range of clinical variables relevant to matching considerations. The six assessment dimensions are: (1) intoxication and withdrawal, (2) biomedical complications, (3) emotional and behavioral complications, (4) treatment resistance, (5) relapse potential, and (6) environmental factors that are not supportive of recovery. The decision-making process outlined in the PPC is detailed enough to allow for a standardized implementation of the assessment process.[12]

It is a well-established concern in substance abuse research and treatment that subjects and patients are not necessarily consistent (reflecting reliability) or accurate (reflecting validity) in their reporting of problems and behaviors. Babor et al.[13,14] have proposed a heuristic social-psychological model of data collection in the interview process which states that assessments may introduce multiple potential sources of error. Investigations may introduce error in relation to both the subject and the assessment situation. Error may be introduced from characteristics that are relatively stable, such as cultural background, cognitive ability and the nature of the assessment questions. Inaccuracies may also result from factors that vary across time and situations, such as subject motivation and, where multiple interviewers are involved, the style and characteristics of the interviewers.

The development of a comprehensive system of treatment planning in substance abuse is a challenging task. The decision tree must integrate medical, psychological, behavioral and environmental data relating to all the categories of the drugs of abuse and their routes of use in what is essentially a mathematical or logic formula. Validity concerns aside, such as system is rife with opportunity for imprecision, misinterpretation, distortion and other sources of inaccuracy. In developing a standardized assessment of the PPC and demonstrating that it can be implemented to yield a reliable assignment to LOC, these multiple sources of error must be considered. A first step in reducing inconsistency certainly involves selecting standardized "feeder" instruments with known reliability and validity to implement the PPC in the ASAM Criteria Validity Study. However, since an equally important source of error involves the thoroughness and consistency with which the assessment protocol is implemented, the training of interviewers to maximize reliability requires as much attention.

Purpose: Our goal in this study was to establish whether and how a standardized protocol could be used by different interviewers to reliably assign subjects to the appropriate LOC. After developing a computerized structured assessment, we determined the inter-rater reliability of the ASAM PPC assessment interview.

METHODS

The Assessment Protocol

The crux of the treatment-matching study has been the development of a standardized assessment protocol that could be used to determine the LOC for which a subject qualifies. Given the number and complexity of both the variables and the decision rules involved, the PPC-1 was subjected to a decision analysis process. In a method published by Turner et al.,[12] the original document was found to specify 121 decisions rules, which, when further deconstructed through decision analysis, yielded 266 discrete decision points that required specific clinical data in order to be solved. Questions from research instruments with known reliability were operationalized by a multidisciplinary clinical panel of the MGH Addiction Research Program. These research question items were used in their original format, and within the context of the original instrument, appearing on the screen of the laptop computer in proper sequence. The original scoring mechanisms were also retained, and threshold levels were set to determine how each item contributes to a particular LOC. For example, an item from the Addiction Severity Index Drug Severity Scale regarding the number of days of drug use during the past thirty would contribute to (although not necessarily dictate) Level-I (outpatient care) if less than 15 (less frequent than every other day) but would contribute to Level-III (residential) or Level-IV (hospital) if 30 (daily use). This approach of using unadulterated, research question items from instruments of known validity offers the best opportunity to achieve reliability.

Items, scoring thresholds and scoring logic were then submitted as a paper version algorithm map for review by an external expert consensus panel selected by ASAM for clinical expertise in the PPC-1. The expert review panel members were recommended by the American Society of Addiction Medicine. Panelists consisted of six practicing psychologists, addiction psychiatrists and addiction medicine specialists who had either participated in the writing or the review of the PPC-1. Panelists were asked to read, for each decision rule of the published PPC-1, each proposed question item, threshold score and algebraic equation that the MGH/Harvard group chose to implement that rule. Panelists were then asked to indicate any questions, disagreements or necessary changes or to indicate if they agreed that the decision rule was accurately interpreted. Extensive comments were provided by the panelists, implemented in a set of revisions, and then re-reviewed for acceptance by the panel.

Finally, a computerized algorithm was constructed which determines the LOC for which a subject qualifies. While the reliability of each of the instruments incorporated into the protocol had already been established, the combining of instruments to create a computerized algorithm represented a unique application that required its own investigation of reliability.

The present study was initiated before the PPC second edition (PPC-2)[5] and the PPC-2 revised edition (PPC-2R)[6] were published and before these latter versions were even conceived. All three versions utilized the same basic format, the same approach to describing LOCs and the identical six dimensions of patient assessment. In this common architecture, the method of implementing and testing PPC-1 serves as a model for all subsequent versions. Some key ways in which PPC-1 differs from the PPC-2 and -2R is that these expand the described LOCs from four in PPC-1 to six major levels with sublevels in PPC-2, and add distinct detoxification levels and dual diagnosis enhanced sublevels in PPC-2R. For example, PPC-2 added levels for Opiate Maintenance Treatment and Early Intervention and Level-II (intensive outpatient care) was divided into day treatment vs. partial hospital. Therefore this study examined only the original four major LOCs and did not test the expanded levels or sublevels of PPC-2 or PPC-2R. Nevertheless, the major levels of Levels II and III in PPC-1 are analogous in the subsequent PPC-2 and PPC-2R. Therefore, this study of the reliability of PPC-1 is applicable and even a necessary pre-requisite for judging the reliability of subsequent versions, since reliability must be established at least for the major LOCs, and only if reliable assessment of these is possible can reliability be expected for the second edition's sub-levels.

Measures

Instruments for the assessment protocol in the ASAM Criteria Validity Study were selected on the basis of their known reliability and validity as well as their relevance to the dimensions that define the PPC-1. The following is a description of the instruments that comprise the assessment protocol.

The Addiction Severity Index (ASI): The ASI[15,16] was selected for its clinical relevance and its well-established psychometric properties. McLellan et al. designed the semi-structured format to assess Medical Status, Employment/Support Status, Drug and Alcohol Use, Legal Status, Family History, Family/Social Relationships, and Psychiatric Status. The composite scores for each dimension have been shown to have both fairly high internal consistency (alphas of .70 or higher) and significant convergent validity with other related measures.[17] In a three-site study, interrater reliability was reported with an average concordance of .89.[17]

The Recovery Attitude and Treatment Evaluator-Clinical Evaluation (RAATE-CE): The RAATE-CE[18,19] is a clinician-rated semi-structured interview developed by some of the authors of the ASAM Patient Placement Criteria to support some essential data requirements of the Criteria. Mee-Lee and Hoffmann designed the RAATE subscales to assess: (A) degree of resistance to treatment, (B) degree of resistance to continuing care, (C) acuity of biomedical problems, (D) acuity of psychiatric problems, and (E) extent of social/family/environmental systems unsupportive of recovery.

Interrater reliability on the original instrument's five RAATE subscales has been reported to range from .59 to .77 in a study of 139 public sector, high severity patients.[20] Interrater reliability was higher with raters who had higher levels of clinical expertise. Validity was studied in 220 consecutive admissions to an inpatient addictions unit with all five RAATE subscales showing one or more associations in the expected direction with subsequent treatment outcomes.[21]

The RAATE-CE/R is an interviewer-administered revision designed for use in research. It provides specific probes for each question and descriptive anchors to explain quantitative ratings. Preliminary reliability data indicate high interrater reliability (.66 to .92 for the five subscales; .88 for the total score), high internal consistency, independence of subscales and a factor structure that partially supports the scale's original design.[22] Validation of the RAATE-CE/R is currently in progress with a sample of 240 patients enrolled in the NIDA Cocaine Collaborative Treatment Study, a randomized psychotherapy outcome trial.[23]

Clinical Institute Withdrawal Assessment-Alcohol/Revised (CIWA-Ar) & Clinical Institute Narcotic Assessment (CINA): The first dimension of the Patient Placement Criteria requires an assessment of the risk associated with the current level of acute intoxication. The CIWA-Ar and its companion, the CINA, are brief scales containing ten items each which provide a clinical quantification of the severity of the alcohol or drug withdrawal syndrome.[24-26] An observer rates the intensity of ten common withdrawal symptoms and a total score is obtained by summing the ratings from the 10 items. With training, these scales have been reliably used by non-medical personnel such as detoxification unit workers or research assistants.[27-29]

Hamilton Depression Rating Scale: A six-item version of the Hamilton Depression Rating Scale was included in the protocol.[30,31] The six-item version was developed from the original version as a more consistent measure of depressive states across different depressive subtypes. It measures depressed mood, guilt, work status, psychomotor retardation, anxiety and somatic symptoms. O'Sullivan et al. investigated the sensitivity of the six-item version against the 17-, 21- and 24-item versions and found that it was comparable for detecting both severity of depression and improvement with treatment. Because of its greater consistency across patient variables and the fact that it takes less time to administer, the six-item version was included to assess for the presence and severity of depressive symptoms.[32]

Mini-Mental Status Exam: The Mini-Mental Status Exam was used as a gross screening of cognitive function.[33] It was designed as a brief screening for dementia to aid differential diagnosis in psychiatric settings. Examples of questions are: "In what way are an arm and a leg alike?" and, "Count backwards from 5 to 1."

Procedures

Interviewer Selection and Training: Interrater reliability on the protocol was assessed for the four interviewers in the ASAM Criteria Validity Study conducted at Massachusetts General Hospital. Based upon the principles outlined by Babor et al.[13,14] and Del Boca et al.[11] regarding the rationale and method for enhancing reliability, careful attention was paid to the selection and training of interviewers, as well as to ongoing monitoring of protocol implementation.

Interviewers were selected on the basis of their educational background, prior clinical exposure and experience with conducting research interviews. Of the four raters, two were master's level counselors, one was a bachelor's level psychology major and one was completing a bachelor's degree with extensive mental health/substance abuse work experience and a background in nursing. All interviewers had prior experience working with substance abuse populations in clinical settings. Three of the four had previously participated as raters or interviewers in research studies and had prior experience with at least some of the instruments used in the assessment protocol.

Training and supervision of the research interviewers was conducted by the senior author who is a clinician as well as a trained and experienced rater on all of the instruments contained in the protocol. Interviewers received specific training on each of the instruments. Training manuals provided to each interviewer contained a copy of each instrument along with background information, administration instructions/manuals and information on how to handle troublesome questions within a given instrument. In addition, each manual included general guidelines for conducting interviews with suggestions for helping subjects to focus, clarifying responses and handling certain forms of resistance.

An initial training seminar was conducted using didactic sessions to complement the written training materials as well as discussion of training videotapes for specific instruments. Interviewers had the opportunity to observe interviews conducted by trained raters and to conduct practice interviews with actual patients. Question/feedback sessions followed the practice interviews.

At the end of the initial training phase, each interviewer was required to undergo a certification process for the individual instruments in which their ratings of standard sets of tapes obtained from previous studies were compared with expert ratings. Using the kappa statistic,[34] interviewers' ratings were evaluated in relation to thresholds established to reflect adequate interrater reliability.

Once certified, interviewers received ongoing supervision from the senior author in relation to protocol implementation. In addition, audio tapes of actual assessments were made by each interviewer and rated by all other interviewers. Group discussion/feedback sessions were then held to clarify areas of discrepancy among interviewers.

Inter-Rater Reliability Study

While the ASAM Criteria Validity Study involves the validation of only the middle two LOCs, the assessment protocol was designed to be implemented across all four LOCs specified in the original ASAM Criteria. It was, therefore, important to design a study that would establish preliminary reliability for the protocol across the full range of treatment intensity.

To accomplish this objective, subjects were recruited from the three intensive ASAM Criteria LOCs, i.e., Level II (day treatment), Level III (nonhospital inpatient) and Level IV (hospital inpatient). The sample of addiction patients from whom target video subjects were drawn did not include Level I (outpatient) due to the design and the exclusion criteria of the ASAM Criteria Validity Study. Subjects were informed of the purpose and nature of the study according to procedures approved by the MGH Institutional Review Board and, if subjects agreed to be videotaped, they underwent the full assessment interview and were paid in gift certificates for their participation. Each interviewer recorded at least three videotaped interviews.

The LOC for which a subject qualified was determined by the computerized algorithm at the completion of the assessment protocol. Eight tapes were selected for the interrater reliability study: two subjects who qualified for Level IV, four who qualified for Level III and two who qualified for Level II. Each of the tapes was viewed and rated by the three remaining raters who were blind to the level to which the subject had been assigned. Raters also were not informed as to which levels were being represented or in what proportion.

RESULTS

Interrater Reliability

Interrater reliability was calculated using an ANOVA intraclass correlation approach[34] so that all raters could be compared with one another. Table 1 shows the intraclass correlation coefficient for ASAM LOC assignment (.77) along with coefficients for each of the instruments and their subscales. With the exception of two of the RAATE subscales, all values were above .70 and all but one were significant at the .05 level or higher, indicating high interrater reliability.

Using the composite scores of the ASI as a means of establishing interrater reliability, it was possible to demonstrate perfect or near perfect agreement (.87 to 1.00) across all four raters. Similarly, the CIWA (.87) and CINA (.92) yielded very high levels of agreement. These results would indicate that it is possible to reliably characterize the various dimensions of substance use severity. The fact that both the Hamilton Depression Rating Scale (.80) and the Mini-Mental Status Exam (.87) reliability coefficients were equally high is evidence that it is also possible to assess aspects of psychological functioning in a reliable manner within a substance abuse assessment protocol.

Overall reliability on the RAATE was high (.88), however, reliability of the RAATE subscales varied widely. In particular, the subscale A–Resistance to Treatment (.22) and subscale D–Psychiatric Acuity (.48) failed to demonstrate adequate interrater reliability. An examination of the coefficient for both subscales revealed that the variance associated with differences across videotapes was relatively small in both cases, indicating that there was little difference among the subjects on the two dimensions. In terms of RAATE Subscale A–Resistance to Treatment, this finding is not surprising, given that subjects were all treatment-seeking and sufficiently motivated to volunteer for research interviews. On RAATE Subscale C–Psychiatric Acuity it is possible that exclusion criteria for consent procedures also led to limited variability across

TABLE 1. Intraclass Correlation Coefficients for the ASAM Assessment Protocol by Instrument and LOC Assignment

Instrument	ICC (*significance)
ASI	
Medical Composite	1.00***
Employment Composite	.96***
Alcohol Composite	1.00***
Drug Composite	1.00***
Legal Composite	.92***
Family Composite	.87***
Psychiatric Composite	1.00***
RAATE	
Resistance to Treatment	.22
Resistance to Continuing Care	.80***
Biomedical Problems	.88***
Psychiatric Problems	.48*
Environmental Obstacles	.73**
Total Score	.88***
CIWA	.87***
CINA	.92***
Hamilton Depression Scale	.80***
Mini-Mental Status	.87***
ASAM LOC Assignment	.77**

$*p < .05$ $**p < .01$ $***p < .001$

tapes. The impact in both cases was to create a ceiling effect which attenuated the variance, thereby negatively impacting the intraclass correlation coefficient.

DISCUSSION

The primary aim of the study was to establish the viability of implementing a standardized assessment protocol for assigning patients to the appropriate LOC according to the PPC-1. Protocol implementation was subjected to a test of interrater reliability using videotaped interviews and trained interviewers. The results were promising in that overall, interrater reliability was high, both for the established "feeder" instruments and for the LOC assignment. It should be pointed out that the achievement of interrater reliability for LOC assignment was not a simple and direct consequence of establishing reliability for the individual instruments. The algorithm was constructed in such a way as to rely upon individual items from within the instruments. This made the task considerably more difficult, as raters can vary on a given individual item and still achieve relatively high levels of reliability on a subscale or total score. However, to the extent that an item with poor reliability was selected for the algorithm, it had the potential to negatively impact the reliability of level assignment in a manner that would be exaggerated compared to high subscale interrater reliability on the individual instruments. Thus, it is not surprising that reliability for the ASAM LOC, though adequate, was not as high as for the original instruments that served as sources for feeder items to the PPC-1 algorithm.

RAATE-CE-R subscales from the current study were compared with those of Najavits et al.[22] using the same research version of the RAATE. Overall, interrater reliability was nearly identical in both studies, with entirely different cohorts of raters. However, on some subscales, reliability in the current study was somewhat lower than the previous report (Subscale A .22 vs. .66, Subscale D .48 vs. .84, Subscale E .73 vs. .92), whereas on others reliability in the current study was actually higher (Subscale B .80 vs. .67, Subscale C .88 vs. .84).

Comparison of Interrater Reliability

Studies of other diagnostic and global measures place our results in context. In diagnostic classification, interrater reliability has been fairly extensively studied. Data on both the Diagnostic and Statistical Manual 3rd edition, revised or 4th edition (DSM III-R or DSM IV) and the International Classification of Disease 10th edition (ICD-10) offer some perspective on the degree of reliability that has been found for substance use disorder diagnoses. Although a direct comparison with intraclass correlations is not possible, it is helpful to look at kappa scores for these categorical diagnoses.

Using the Structured Clinical Interview for DSM III-R (SCID), Skre et al.[35] obtained a kappa of .96 for alcohol abuse or dependence and .85 for other (illegal or prescription drug) abuse or dependence. It should be noted that raters did not have to distinguish abuse from dependence in these ratings. In the NIDA Cocaine Collaborative Treatment Study, using the SCID for DSM IV, kappas for Alcohol Dependence, Substance-Induced Mood Disorder and Antisocial Personality Disorder were .82, .73 and .67, respectively (Moras, 1997 personal communication). In the ICD-10 field trials, Regier et al.[36] used a defined protocol with two raters, with agreement for the two-digit diagnosis of psychoactive substance use disorders yielding a kappa of .82. For the three-digit diagnosis of alcohol use disorders, kappa was .82 and for the four-digit diagnoses it dropped off, with a kappa of .61 for alcohol dependence and only .33 for alcohol–harmful use. These results would indicate that the greater the specificity with which a diagnosis is made, the more difficult it is to establish reliability. Given that the ASAM LOC Assignment attempts not only to identify a problem but to quantify it with some specificity, it would appear to be doing so with more than respectable reliability.

A widely used measure of overall severity of psychiatric disturbance is the Global Assessment Scale (GAS),[37] a modified version of which was included in DSM III-R as the Global Assessment of Functioning (GAF) Scale. Endicott et al.'s original data on the psychometric properties of the scale included five interrater reliability studies for which intraclass correlations of .61, .69, .76, .85, and .91 were reported across a range of populations.[37] In the present study, the ASAM LOC Assignment intraclass correlation of .77 is thus clearly in the same range as these scores. A recent study by Hall[38] comparing the original GAS with the modified GAF with the same sample using trained raters reported intraclass correlations of .62 and .81, respectively, indicating that the modified scale may offer higher reliability. However, a study using the GAF with untrained raters in mental health settings yielded an intraclass correlation of .54, which failed to reach statistical significance, indicating the importance of training in its widespread implementation.

The initial process of establishing interrater reliability for the ASAM LOC assignment, though promising, is also instructive in terms of future needs for refinement. The fact that two of the RAATE subscales performed poorly requires further consideration. Were it solely a training issue, it would not be expected that only isolated subscales would be so negatively impacted. A more detailed examination of intraclass correlation coefficients revealed that in each case, there were individual items that accounted for most of the discrepancies. Given that the construction of the algorithm relies upon individual items, it would stand to reason that where these items with poor reliability were included in the algorithm, reliability for LOC assignment was negatively impacted.

Publication of the PPC represents an ambitious effort to integrate diverse types of clinical data into a comprehensive treatment matching decision tree. Given the limited evidence for treatment matching by single-model behavioral therapies,[2,3] the alternative ASAM Criteria model, i.e., matching by integrated medical and psychosocial decision rules into multi-modality treatment settings, may show greater validity.[1] With over 15,000 volumes of the PPC sold, the utility of these protocols for standardizing addictions care lies in doubt if the potential for reliability is not assured. This study strongly supports the notion of a standardized, multi-instrument assessment protocol for establishing the ASAM LOC. It demonstrates that using available instruments, interviewers can be trained to be consistent in the implementation of a multi-instrument assessment protocol. The mean duration of administration, reported elsewhere as 58 minutes, is a further reflection of feasibility.[12] These results, in a complex disease domain such as substance abuse, are encouraging. With further refinement of both the algorithm and the training process there is reason to expect that even higher levels of reliability can be achieved. Further such efforts at refinement are underway in the ASAM Criteria Validity Study.

REFERENCES

1. Gastfriend DR, McLellan AT. Treatment matching: Theoretic basis and practical implications. Med Clin N Amer. 1997;81(4):945-966.

2. Project MATCH Research Group. Matching alcoholism treatment to client heterogeneity: Project MATCH posttreatment drinking outcomes. J Stud Alcohol. 1997; 58(1):7-29.

3. Ouimette PC, Finney JW, Gima K, Moos RH. A comparative evaluation of substance abuse treatment III. Examining mechanisms underlying patient-treatment matching hypotheses for 12-step and cognitive-behavioral treatments for substance abuse. Alcohol Clin Exp Res. 1999;23(3):545-551.

4. Hoffmann N, Halikas J, Mee-Lee D, Weedman R. American Society of Addiction Medicine–Patient Placement Criteria for the treatment of psychoactive substance use disorders. 1st ed. Washington, DC: ASAM, 1991.

5. American Society of Addiction Medicine. Patient placement criteria for the treatment of substance-related disorders. Second Edition ed. Chevy Chase, MD: American Society of Addiction Medicine, Inc., 1996.

6. Mee-Lee D, Shulman GD, Fishman M, et al., eds. ASAM Patient Placement Criteria for the Treatment of Substance-Related Disorders, Second Edition–Revised

(ASAM PPC-2R). Chevy Chase, MD: American Society of Addiction Medicine, Inc., 2001.

7. Center for Substance Abuse Treatment. The Role and Current Status of Patient Placement Criteria in the Treatment of Substance Use Disorders. Treatment Improvement Protocol (TIP). Rockville, MD: Substance Abuse and Mental Health Services Administration, 1995.

8. Morey L. Patient placement criteria: Linking typologies to managed care. Alc Health & Rsh Wld. 1996;20(1):36-44.

9. Book J, Harbim H, Marques C, et. al. The ASAM's and Green Spring's alcohol and drug detoxification and rehabilitation criteria for utilization review. Am J Addiction. 1995;4(3):187-197.

10. McKay JR, Cacciola JS, McLellan AT, et al. An initial evaluation of the psychosocial dimensions of the American Society of Addiction Medicine criteria for inpatient vs. intensive outpatient substance abuse rehabilitation. J Stud Alcohol. 1997;58(5):239-252.

11. Del Boca FK, Babor TF, McRee B. Reliability enhancement and estimation in multisite clinical trials. J Stud Alcohol. 1994;12:130-136.

12. Turner WM, Turner KH, Reif S, et al. Feasibility of multidimensional substance abuse treatment matching: Automating the ASAM Patient Placement Criteria . Drug Alc Depend. 1999;55:35-43.

13. Babor T, Stephens R, Marlatt G. Verbal report methods in clinical research on alcoholism: Response bias and its minimization. J Stud Alcohol. 1987;48:410-424.

14. Babor T, Brown I, Del Boca F. Fact or fiction? Behavioral Assessment. 1990;12:5-31.

15. McLellan AT, Luborsky L, Woody GE. An improved diagnostic evaluation instrument for substance abuse patients: The Addiction Severity Index. Journal of Nervous and Mental Disease. 1980;168:26-33.

16. McLellan A, Kushner H, Metzger M, et al. The fifth edition of the Addiction Severity Index. J Subst Abuse Treat. 1992;9:199-213.

17. McLellan A, Luborsky L, Cacciola J, et al. New data from the Addiction Severity Index-Reliability and validity in three centers. J Nerv Mental Dis. 1985;173(7): 412-423.

18. Mee-Lee D. The Recovery Attitude and Treatment Evaluator (RAATE) an instrument for patient progress and treatment assignment. Proceedings of the 34th International Congress on Alcoholism and Drug Dependence. Calgary, Alberta; 1985: 424-426.

19. Mee-Lee D. An instrument for treatment progress and matching: The Recovery Attitude and Treatment Evaluator (RAATE). J Subst Abuse Treatment. 1988;5(3): 183-186.

20. Smith M, Hoffman N, Nederhoed R. The development and reliability of the RAATE-CE. J Subst Abuse. 1992;4:355-363.

21. Gastfriend DR, Filstead WJ, Reif S, et al. Validity of assessing treatment readiness in patients with substance use disorders. Am J Addiction. 1995;4(3):254-260.

22. Najavits LM, Gastfriend DR, Nakayama EY, et al. A measure of readiness for substance abuse treatment: Psychometric properties of the RAATE research interview. Am J Addiction. 1997;6(1):74-82.

23. Crits-Christoph P, Siqueland L, Blaine J, et al. The National Institute on Drug Abuse Collaborative Cocaine Treatment Study. Rationale and methods. Arch Gen Psychiatry. 1997;54(8):721-726.

24. Sullivan JT, Sykora K, Schneiderman J, et al. Assessment of alcohol withdrawal: The revised Clinical Institute Withdrawal Assessment for Alcohol Scale. Br J Addict. 1989;84:1353-1357.

25. Fudala PJ, Berkow LC, Fralich JL, Johnson RE. Use of naloxone in the assessment of opiate dependence. Life Sci. 1991;49(24):1809-1814.

26. Peachey J, Lei H. Assessment of opioid dependence with naloxone. Br J Addict. 1988;83(2):193-201.

27. Wartenberg AA, Nirenberg TD, Liepman MR, et al. Detoxification of alcoholics: Improving care by symptom-triggered sedation. Alcohol Clin Exp Res. 1990; 14(1):71-75.

28. Saitz R, Mayo Smith MF, Roberts MS, et al. Individualized treatment for alcohol withdrawal: A randomized double-blind controlled trial. Journal of the American Medical Association 1994;272(7):519-523.

29. Wasilewski D, Matsumoto H, Kur E, et al. Assessment of diazepam loading dose therapy of delirium tremens. Alcohol Alcohol. 1996;31(3):273-278.

30. Hamilton M. A rating scale for depression. J Neurol Neurosur Psychiat. 1960;23:56-62.

31. Bech P, Allerup P, Gram L, et al. The Hamilton Depression Scale. Acta Psyc Scandi. 1981;63:290-299.

32. O'Sullivan R, Fava M, Agustin C, et al. Sensitivity of the 6 item Hamilton Depression Rating Scale. Acta Psych Scandi. 1997;95(5):379-384.

33. Folstein MF, Folstein SE, McHugh PR. "Mini-mental state." A practical method for grading the cognitive state of patients for the clinician. J Psychiatr Res. 1975;12:189-198.

34. Bartko JH, Carpenter WT. On the methods and theory of reliability. The Journal of Nervous and Mental Disease. 1976;163(5):307-317.

35. Skre I, Onstad S, Edvardsen J, et al. A family study of anxiety disorders: Familial transmission and relationship to mood disorder and psychoactive substance use disorder. Acta Psychiatr Scand. 1994;90:366-374.

36. Regier DA, Kaebler CT, Roper MT, et al. The ICD-10 clinical field trial for mental and behavioral disorders: Results in Canada and the United States. Am J Psychiatry. 1994;151:1340-1350.

37. Endicott J, Spitzer R, Fleiss J, Cohen J. The Global Assessment Scale: A procedure for measuring overall severity of psychiatric diagnosis. Arch Gen Psychiatry. 1976;33:766-773.

38. Hall R. Global assessment of functioning: A modified scale. Psychosomatics 1995;36:267-275.

Convergent Validity
of the ASAM Patient Placement Criteria
Using a Standardized Computer Algorithm

Graham Staines, PhD
Nicole Kosanke, PhD
Stephen Magura, PhD, CSW
Priti Bali, BA
Jeffrey Foote, PhD
Alexander Deluca, MD

SUMMARY. The study examined the convergent validity of the ASAM Patient Placement Criteria (PPC) by comparing Level of Care (LOC)

Graham Staines, Nicole Kosanke, Stephen Magura, and Priti Bali are affiliated with the Institute for Treatment and Services Research, National Development and Research Institutes, New York, NY.

Jeffrey Foote was affiliated with the Smithers Treatment Center, St. Lukes-Roosevelt Medical Center, New York, NY at time of the study. Dr. Foote is currently at the National Center on Addiction and Substance Abuse, Columbia University, New York, NY.

Alexander Deluca was affiliated with Smithers Treatment Center, St. Lukes-Roosevelt Medical Center, New York, NY at time of the study. Dr. DeLuca is currently in private practice, New York, NY.

Address correspondence to: Dr. Stephen Magura, NDRI, 71 West 23rd Street, New York, NY 10010 (E-mail: magura@ndri.org).

This study was supported by grant no. R01AA10863 from the National Institute on Alcohol Abuse and Alcoholism to Dr. Magura.

An earlier version of this paper was presented at the American Society of Addiction Medicine (ASAM) 31st Annual Medical-Scientific Conference, Chicago, Illinois, April 15, 2000.

[Haworth co-indexing entry note]: "Convergent Validity of the ASAM Patient Placement Criteria Using a Standardized Computer Algorithm." Staines, Graham et al.. Co-published simultaneously in *Journal of Addictive Diseases* (The Haworth Medical Press, an imprint of The Haworth Press, Inc.) Vol. 22, Supplement No. 1, 2003, pp. 61-77; and: *Addiction Treatment Matching: Research Foundations of the American Society of Addiction Medicine (ASAM) Criteria* (ed: David R. Gastfriend) The Haworth Medical Press, an imprint of The Haworth Press, Inc., 2003, pp. 61-77. Single or multiple copies of this article are available for a fee from The Haworth Document Delivery Service [1-800-HAWORTH, 9:00 a.m. - 5:00 p.m. (EST). E-mail address: docdelivery@haworthpress.com].

Digital Object Identifier: 10.1300/J069v22S01_05

recommendations produced by two alternative methods: a computer-driven algorithm and a "standard" clinical assessment. A cohort of 248 applicants for alcoholism treatment were evaluated at a multi-modality treatment center. The two methods disagreed (58% of cases) more often than they agreed (42%). The algorithm recommended a more intense LOC than the clinician protocol in 81% of the discrepant cases. Four categories of disagreement accounted for 97% of the discrepant cases. Several major sources of disagreement were identified and examined in detail: clinicians' reasoned departures from the PPC rules, conservatism in algorithm LOC recommendations, and measurement overlap between two specific dimensions. In order for the ASAM PPC and its associated algorithm to be embraced by treatment programs, the observed differences in LOC recommendations between the algorithm and "standard" clinical assessment should be resolved. *[Article copies available for a fee from The Haworth Document Delivery Service: 1-800-HAWORTH. E-mail address: <docdelivery@haworthpress.com> Website: <http://www.HaworthPress. com> © 2003 by The Haworth Press, Inc. All rights reserved.]*

KEYWORDS. ASAM Criteria, treatment matching algorithm, substance abuse assessment, convergent validity, computer decision assistance

INTRODUCTION

There is widespread interest among community programs, treatment funders and insurers in using standardized patient placement criteria (PPC) to match addicted patients to the appropriate placement or *level of care (LOC)*, i.e, the treatment setting, treatment intensity, and mix of services most suitable for each patient's needs.[1] The American Society of Addiction Medicine (ASAM) PPC are arguably the most prominent set of professionally developed practice guidelines for matching addiction patients to putatively suitable levels of care.[2-4] The original ASAM Criteria (PPC-1) identified and described four principal levels of treatment: Level 1 (Outpatient Treatment), Level 2 (Intensive Outpatient/ Partial Hospitalization Treatment), Level 3 (Medically-Monitored Intensive Inpatient Treatment, i.e., residential treatment), and Level 4 (Medically-Managed Intensive Inpatient Treatment, i.e., hospitalization). The criteria in this consensus document allowed clinicians to evaluate the severity of a patient's need for treatment along six dimensions: (1) Acute intoxication and/or withdrawal potential; (2) Biomedical conditions and complications; (3) Emotional/behavioral conditions;

(4) Treatment acceptance/resistance; (5) Relapse potential; and (6) Recovery environment. Further, the ASAM Criteria specified rules for combining the scores on each dimension to generate an overall recommendation for the appropriate LOC for each patient. The original ASAM Criteria have subsequently been revised and updated twice (PPC-2, PPC-2R).[3,5]

Because the complexity of using the ASAM PPC challenges even the most experienced clinicians, Gastfriend and colleagues[6,7] developed a reliable computerized decision-making algorithm to integrate all relevant information for recommending levels of care as required by the original ASAM Criteria (PPC-1).

Study Purpose: The present study, which is part of a broader longitudinal study of the ASAM Criteria, explores issues pertinent to the practical use of the ASAM PPC. The purpose of the study is to assess the convergent validity of the original ASAM PPC-1 by comparing the results of two alternative procedures for determining a patient's level of care. These procedures are the computer-driven algorithm and a "standard" clinical assessment. The study determines the degree of agreement between the algorithm-based and clinician-based recommendations for level of care. Further, the patterns of disagreement and reasons for disagreement are examined. Implications of the results for the current version of the Criteria (PPC-2R)[5] and revised algorithm (work in progress) will be discussed.

METHODS

Participants: Study subjects were alcohol dependent/abusing patients (determined by DSM-IV diagnosis utilizing the Structured Clinical Interview for DSM-IV [SCID]) who presented for treatment at Smithers Treatment Center, St. Lukes-Roosevelt Hospital, New York, NY. The sample included patients who were newly accepted for inpatient or outpatient treatment and also those who had been discharged from detoxification or residential care and were applying for continuing treatment. Applicants initially screened by Smithers medical staff and then referred for hospital detoxification (Level IV) at other facilities were not included in the study; Smithers did not have Level IV treatment available. Only a small number of applicants were not accepted for treatment at Smithers because of behavioral risks (violent behavior, threats, suicidality, etc.) and consequently did not enter the study.

Eligible applicants were approached and invited to participate in the study in order of their appearance at the program on any specific day that interviewing occurred. Research staff availability determined the number of interviews conducted each day. The baseline study sample consists of 248 applicants who were interviewed and entered treatment between April 1998 and September 1999.

Setting and Procedures: Smithers accepts patients who have an addiction problem, with public or private insurance coverage as well as self-pay status. During the study period Smithers offered treatment programs at three levels of care (LOC) as defined by the ASAM Criteria: Regular Outpatient (Level I: 2 sessions per week of 1.5 hours each); Intensive Outpatient (Level II: 5 sessions per week of 3.5 hours each); and Inpatient Rehabilitation (Level III: 28 day maximum). The study was located at the Smithers Evaluation Unit, where the study's baseline interviews were conducted as an extension of the regular intake assessment process. These extended interviews, which averaged 2.5 hours, included the algorithm's "feeder" instruments such as the Addiction Severity Index (ASI) and the Recovery Attitude and Treatment Evaluation (RAATE).[7]

Whereas the algorithm generated scores on the six ASAM Criteria dimensions and an overall recommendation for level of care, the clinicians determined a level of care based on the ASAM Criteria by conducting their own regular intake interviews, as well as having access to data collected through the algorithm feeder instruments. The second procedure we term the "standard clinical assessment." The clinicians did not know the algorithm's level of care recommendation either before making their own recommendations or before trying to implement their placement recommendations.

Sample Characteristics: The 248 subjects included a mix of working- and middle-class patients, as well as those more socioeconomically disadvantaged. The majority were male (72%); African-American (44%) or white (35%); high school graduates (77%); never married (46%) or separated, widowed, or divorced (34%); and their average age was 40. The percent diagnosed as both alcohol dependent/abusing and drug dependent/abusing was 64%.

Sample Representativeness: To test for sample bias, the study sample (N = 248) was compared with 633 other applicants who presented at Smithers during the data collection period and met the study's eligibility criteria, but who did not participate. Clinic records data on 10 key patient attributes indicate no significant differences between participants and eligible nonparticipants.

RESULTS

Algorithm-Derived vs. Clinician-Derived Level of Care (LOC): Table 1 presents a cross-tabulation comparing the level of care recommendations from the algorithm (ALG LOC) with those from clinicians (CLIN LOC). Most of the cases were assigned different levels of care by the algorithm and the clinicians: 58% discrepant cases (based on 9 off-diagonal cells in the table) vs. 42% congruent cases (based on the 3 bolded diagonal cells). Note there were no clinician recommendations of Level IV.

For most of the discrepant cases, the algorithm recommended higher levels of care, i.e., was more restrictive, than the clinicians: 81% of cases algorithm higher vs. 19% of cases clinicians higher. Four categories accounted for 97% of the discrepancies: (1) ALG LOC=IV but CLIN LOC<IV (49 cases); (2) ALG LOC=III but CLIN LOC=II (29 cases); (3) ALG LOC=II but CLIN LOC=I (37 cases); and (4) ALG LOC=II but CLIN LOC=III (25 cases). ALG LOC was higher than CLIN LOC for the first three categories but lower for the fourth, i.e., more permissive.

To analyze the discrepancies in each of these four major categories, those attributable to departures by the clinicians from the ASAM PPC rules for level of care assignment ("PPC rule departures") were distinguished from discrepancies that were attributable to differences between the algorithm and clinicians in how best to operationalize, i.e., measure and interpret, certain ASAM PPC constructs ("PPC measurement disagreements").

TABLE 1. Level of Care (LOC) Recommendations–Algorithm vs. Clinician

| | Algorithm-Based LOC | | | | |
	I. Regular Outpatient	II. Intensive Outpatient	III. Inpatient Rehabilitation	IV. Hospitalization	Total
Clinician-Based LOC	Total				
I. Regular Outpatient	**5 (2%)**	37 (15%)	2 (1%)	4 (1%)	48 (19%)
II. Intensive Outpatient	2 (1%)	**52 (21%)**	29 (12%)	18 (8%)	101 (41%)
III. Inpatient Rehabilitation	1 (.5%)	25 (10%)	**46 (19%)**	27 (11%)	99 (40%)
Total	8 (3%)	114 (46%)	77 (31%)	49 (20%)	248 (100%)

Note: Bolded entries are congruent.

ALG LOC=IV & CLIN LOC<IV: There were 49 cases (34% of all discrepancies) where the algorithm yielded a recommendation of Level IV, medically-managed inpatient treatment (hospitalization), whereas the standard clinical assessment recommended no Level IV. Note that all applicants to Smithers are screened by medical staff to determine the need for hospitalization (e.g., detoxification); only applicants determined not to require immediate hospitalization were referred for evaluation by the study. We will examine how this large number of discrepant LOC recommendations occurred.

The PPC-1 rule is that a score of "IV" on any of the first three PPC dimensions justifies a placement recommendation of Level IV. The number of cases with a dimensional score of "IV" was 24 for dimension 1, 30 for dimension 2, and 13 for dimension 3. Thirty-three of the cases qualified on only one of the three dimensions, 14 qualified on two dimensions, and two qualified on all three. Only a few criteria or indicators were responsible for most of the algorithm's Level IV recommendations. We examined the criteria and algorithm items by which these applicants were designated as Level IV and determined whether this recommendation might be clinically justified in view of the particulars of each case. Table 2 summarizes these results.

On dimension 1, four physiological/biological indicators, i.e., high systolic blood pressure (> 150, 9 cases), high pulse rate (> 100, 7 cases), and pregnancy (3 cases), each sufficient for the algorithm to generate a recommendation of Level 4, accounted for 19 of the 24 Level IV cases.

TABLE 2. Dimensions and Measures Contributing to ALG LOC = Level IV

	Dimension 1				
	Blood Pressure	Pulse	Pregnancy	Others	Total Cases-Dim 1
Not Clinically Justified	9	7	3	6	24
Possibly Justified	0	0	0	0	0
Total Cases	9	6	3	6	24
	Dimensions 2 and 3				
	ASI Medical Composite	Other	Total Dim 2 Cases	Total Dim 3 Cases	Grand Total
Not Clinically Justified	19	10	29	12	47
Possibly Justified	0	1	1	1	2
Total Cases	19	11	30	13	49

Such physiological indicators, clinicians pointed out, would require hospitalization only if there were additional reasons why detoxification, if needed, could not be managed safely in a lower level of care, e.g., a substantial risk of severe withdrawal symptoms or acute illness. Retrospective examination of the patient interviews and charts did not indicate such circumstances requiring hospitalization.

Among the 30 applicants scoring "IV" on dimension 2, 19 qualified on the basis of their ASI Medical Composite score, which consists of three self-reported items receiving equal weight in the algorithm: "number of days in the last 30 that you were bothered by medical problems," rating of "how troubled or bothered were you by these problems," and rating of "how important to you is treatment for these problems?" This composite is intended as one measure of the PPC dimension 2 criteria relating to biomedical complications of substance use severe enough to require inpatient medical management during detoxification; the threshold score for Level IV was 0.75 out of a potential 1.00.

Almost all of these applicants gave plausible answers to these questions, but the particular medical problems to which they were referring did not appear sufficiently serious or acute to warrant immediate hospitalization (e.g, chronic rather than acute asthma, hypertension, or diabetes). Most of these applicants were on medications for their conditions, but some were not. The Smithers medical staff did not regard any of these applicants as requiring hospitalization, but considered the problems currently manageable in lower levels of care. Examination of the post-admission records for these patients did not indicate any subsequent remarkable medical events, with the exception of an HIV positive patient who developed AIDS during the first month of treatment and was hospitalized.

Eleven additional patients were scored as "IV" on the basis of certain measures of dimension 2 criteria other than the ASI Medical Composite. These measures were, respectively, "Do changes in medical status make abstinence imperative?" "Would continued use of substances jeopardize physical health?" or "Substance use greatly complicates medical condition." Although the questions were "correctly" answered in the affirmative by the interviewer, the literal responses were often misleading because three of these applicants had just completed an inpatient detoxification, thus there was no need to re-hospitalize them to deal with potential biomedical consequences of substance use.

There were 13 cases designated for Level IV by the algorithm based on dimension 3 criteria ('Emotional and Behavioral Conditions and Complications'). Level IV was attained most frequently by the interviewer's rating of whether or not the patient "was having trouble comprehending, concentrating, or remembering" during the interview (five cases), which measured the PPC criterion of "mental confusion/fluctuating orientation." Other indicators that attained Level IV on dimension 3 were: a Hamilton Depression Scale score > 12 (measuring the PPC-1 criterion of "extreme depression"); a Modified Mini-Mental Status Examination score of < 23 (measuring the PPC-1 criterion of "thought process impairment . . . "); and the interviewer's rating that "alcohol/drug use gravely exacerbates a psychiatric or emotional/behavioral condition" (essentially the same wording as a PPC-1 criterion).

Retrospective examination of these 13 cases indicates that hospitalization for initial treatment might have been justified in only one case. According to the interviewer's notes, despite coming directly out of inpatient detoxification, one applicant was "still tremulous" and his mental status "seems foggy." The remaining 12 applicants, while evidencing psychological problems, did not appear to require hospitalization for safety or adequate treatment; most were already receiving psychiatric medication or could obtain it in a lower level of care.

Seventeen of the applicants designated as Level IV by the algorithm had recently been discharged from inpatient alcohol/drug detoxification at various local facilities. Virtually all these discharged patients had been abstinent for five days or longer and thus not at withdrawal risk. Twelve of these 17 were designated for Level IV based on the ASI Medical Composite score.

ALG LOC=III & CLIN LOC=II: There were 29 cases (20% of all discrepancies) where the algorithm recommended inpatient rehabilitation (Level III), but the clinicians recommended intensive outpatient (Level II). The crux of these discrepancies was that the algorithm assigned values of (Level) "III" to dimension 5 (Relapse Prevention) and/or dimension 6 (Recovery Environment), whereas the clinicians assigned values of (Level) "II" to each. This pattern of scores, i.e., "III" from the algorithm, "II" from the clinicians, was evident in 23 cases for dimension 6, in 18 cases for dimension 5, and in 16 cases for both dimensions.

These discrepancies involved almost exclusively measurement issues–differences in the selection and interpretation of indicators to measure the dimensional criteria. The discrepancies are attributable to the clinicians' reliance on "balance," i.e., use of information from multiple items and sources helps to produce a balanced recommendation, as will be seen in the interpretation of dimension 6; on "context," i.e., the use of contextual information to tailor recommendations to specific circumstances, as will be seen in the interpretation of dimension 5; and avoidance of dimensional "overlap," i.e., certain overlap in the operational-ization of dimensions 5 and 6 by the algorithm that led to higher level of care recommendations.

The key items generating the higher algorithm level of care recommendations were four ratings from the RAATE (E1, E2, E3, & E5), which directly pertained to dimension 6, and one overlapping item (E5), which also measured dimension 5. These items are intended to measure the following PPC-1 criterion for Level 3 on Dimension 6: "The patient lives in an environment (social and interpersonal network) in which treatment is unlikely to succeed (e.g., a chaotic family, rife with inter-personal conflict, which undermines patient's efforts to change; or family members and/or significant others living with the patient manifest current substance use disorders and are likely to undermine the patient's recovery)."

E1 rates the degree of family support; E2 rates the degree of sub-stance use among the patient's friends and the recovery-support friends are likely to provide; E3 rates degree to which patient's family is willing to participate in treatment; and E5 rates the level of substance use in pa-tient's environment (home and neighborhood).

Issues of Balance: Twenty-seven of the 29 cases in this discrepancy category received a score of "III" from the algorithm on dimension 6. The algorithm allows two routes to a score of "III" on dimension 6 based on the four RAATE items E1, E2, E3, and E5. The first is an aver-age score of at least 3 on the four items. This approach tended to be ac-ceptable to the clinicians because it attempts to "balance" multiple relevant considerations.

The second route is a score of "IV" on any of these four items. This latter approach was unacceptable to the clinicians because it gives de-terminative weight to only one environmental factor, and in fact the al-gorithm and the clinicians were likely to disagree if a case followed the second route exclusively.

More specifically, the clinicians in this study interpreted the spirit of the above PPC-1 criterion to imply that the environment taken as a whole makes outpatient treatment unlikely to succeed. In other words, a patient's friends, family, and living environment are considered to-gether when determining whether outpatient treatment would be feasi-ble. For example, an "absent or dysfunctional" family (E1 = 4) by itself will not result in an immediate Level III recommendation by the clini-cian because the applicant may have sober friends (E2 = 1 or 2) which would also be taken into account.

Four of the 27 cases with a score of "III" by the algorithm on dimension 6 followed the single item (i.e., second) route only; none qualified via the averaging (i.e., first) route only; 15 cases qualified via both routes; and the remaining 8 cases qualified on the basis of measures other than these four RAATE items.

Issues of Context: The clinicians did not believe that the algorithm-specified scores of "III" or "IV" on one RAATE item (i.e., E5) justified assigning a "III" on dimension 5. There were 23 cases where the algorithm assigned a score of "III" on dimension 5, which for 22 cases was attributable to a score of "III" or "IV" on item E5 alone. These 22 cases qualified for a Level III recommendation exclusively on this basis.

The clinicians contended that the algorithm's selection of items should be relative to the patient's experiences and expectations in his/her local setting, and that item E5 was insufficiently sensitive to situational context. By virtue of living in New York City alone, most study patients qualified for E5 = 3 ("much alcohol or drugs are present" in environment) or E5 = 4 rating ("drug-infested neighborhood or multiple users in environment"). Using this factor alone to exclude patients from outpatient care would severely restrict outpatient care in New York City and inner cities generally, and, moreover, is not justified by the existing research base, which does not show that this factor alone is determinative of outpatient treatment outcomes.

Similarly, the clinicians believed that the algorithm underestimated the importance of contextual factors in assessing dimension 6. The importance of the social environment (i.e., presence/absence of social contacts, substance abuse disorders among family/significant others) depends on the patient's drinking or "using" context. The presence of sobriety in a patient's social contacts is mediated by factors such as: whether the patient uses/drinks alone or with others, and whether the patient has conventional structure in his/her life. For example, living in a Single Room Occupancy (SRO) setting puts patients more at risk if their addictive pattern is to use alone. Likewise, unemployment is less of a risk if patients have other structuring activities in their lives, such as volunteering, non-using family (or community) activities, hobbies, etc.

Issues of Overlap: PPC-1 (and thus the algorithm) requires scores of "III" on any two of the six PPC dimensions to produce an overall recommendation of Level III. Any overlap between the measures of dimensions 5 and 6 could produce scores of Level III on two dimensions that were not independent, and thus inappropriately trigger an overall Level III assignment. One source of overlap was the use of a RAATE item (E5) for the determination of scores on both dimensions. Among the 21 cases with scores of "III" on both dimensions, eight qualified on the basis of E5 = 4; two of the eight qualified exclusively on this basis. Indeed, the clinicians reported difficulty in viewing these two dimensions as wholly independent, since personal controls and environment interact in complex ways that are difficult to "separate" in practice.

ALG LOC=II But CLIN LOC=I: There were 37 cases (25% of all discrepancies) where the algorithm recommended intensive outpatient treatment, but the clinicians recommended regular outpatient. Although most (62%) of the discrepancies concerned measurement issues, some (38%) were related to PPC-1 rules for combining dimensional scores. The discrepancies due to measurement issues usually involved the RAATE items measuring dimension 6 discussed earlier (i.e., E1, E-2, E-3, and E-5). According to the algorithm, attaining an average score between "II" and "III" on these four items resulted in a score of "II" on dimension 6. The clinicians believed that these RAATE items produced unduly high scores on dimension 6. The clinicians incorporated additional information to assess the Recovery Environment, especially the ASI Family and Employment sections. Again, the use of additional measures provided them with more balanced, contextual information that reduced dependence on what they viewed as a dubiously simple correspondence between four RAATE items and dimensional scores.

A second source of discrepancy between the algorithm and the clinicians for this category was departures by the clinicians from the PPC-1 rule for combining dimensional scores to produce a recommended level of care. This rule specifies that a score of "II" on any one of dimensions 2 through 6 justifies an overall recommendation of Level II. The clinicians viewed this rule as too restrictive, and therefore overrode the rule (i.e., assigned Level I instead of Level II) in 38% of these discrepant cases.

According to the clinicians, Level II treatment requires a particularly significant life structure change on the patient's part. For example, Level II treatment precludes a regular work schedule, whereas Level I treatment, which can be integrated into the applicant's current schedule without much disruption (including the option of an evening program), permits employed patients to continue to work their regular hours. Thus the clinicians contended that requiring a dramatic shift in a patient's life structure was warranted only if the patient scored at Level II on more than one dimension of problems.

CLIN LOC=III But ALG LOC=II: There were 25 cases (17% of all discrepancies) in which the algorithm recommended intensive outpa-

tient treatment whereas the clinicians recommended inpatient rehabilitation, a higher level of care. The major source of this type discrepancy
(84% of these cases) involved clinician departures from rules governing
combining of dimensional ratings. The other discrepancies involved
measurement issues related to the selection of indicators for PPC criteria (16%).

The particular PPC-1 rule to which the clinicians took exception (but
which the algorithm followed) was the requirement that *two* of the six
dimensions must have a score of "III" before Level III treatment is recommended. The clinicians argued that a single score of "III" on any of
the six dimensions was sufficient to recommend Level III treatment.
The majority of the clinician "overrides" (67%) were based on a score
of "III" on dimension 5 (Relapse Prevention).

According to PPC-1, Relapse Prevention requiring Level III treatment means that a patient is: (a) experiencing an acute crisis with intensification of addiction symptoms and prospect of severe consequences,
despite active participation at a lesser LOC or self-help fellowship,
(b) recognizes excessive use but has been unable to reduce or control it
as long as alcohol/drugs are present, or (c) requires a modality of treatment that necessitates Level III care. The clinicians believed that, based
on criteria (a) and/or (b), the seriousness of the circumstances warranted
an overall Level III recommendation. In one case, for example, the clinician had reason to believe that the patient was lying regarding his use
while currently in an outpatient treatment program. This treatment program, in referring the case to Smithers, reported that the patient had
made no progress and had been suspended from a subway job one
month earlier for a positive drug test.

In general, the clinicians' perception was that one dimension scored
at Level III justified an overall recommendation of Level III–typically,
when a patient's level of psychosocial disintegration warranted a radi-
cal environmental shift. In some cases, patients and their significant
others were on government assistance and substance use jeopardized
custody of children. Such situations are better labeled chronic as opposed to "acute" (an adjective used in PPC-1 in reference to the need for
Level III care); however, the stubborn chronicity itself is perhaps what
calls for a more intensive inpatient intervention.

DISCUSSION

This study examined the convergent validity of the ASAM PPC by
comparing LOC recommendations arrived at by two alternative meth-

ods: a computer-driven algorithm and a "standard" clinical assessment as conducted by the participating program. The two methods disagreed more often than they agreed (58% vs. 42%). Although the study uncovered a wide variety of reasons for observed discrepancies, three major considerations emerged as important for informing future revisions of the ASAM PPC and its associated computer algorithm.

Clinician Departures from ASAM PPC Rules: The clinicians in this study often overrode two of the PPC rules for combining dimensional scores; these rules appear to continue in the most recent version of the ASAM Criteria, PPC-2R. Because the algorithm followed the PPC rules, the resulting discrepancies actually concern the prescriptions of the Criteria rather than the algorithm. The rules from which clinicians departed were: (1) requiring scores of "III" on at least two dimensions to recommend Level III treatment, criticized by the clinicians as too conservative for some cases, an issue that arose within the discrepancy category termed ALG LOC=II, CLIN LOC=III; and (2) allowing a score of "II" on only one dimension to recommend Level II treatment, criticized by the clinicians as too restrictive for some cases, an issue that arose within the discrepancy category termed ALG LOC=II, CLIN LOC=I.

Restrictiveness in Algorithm LOC Recommendations: As compared with the standard clinical assessment, the algorithm showed an overall tendency toward restrictiveness (higher level) recommendations for level of care, as indicated by three of the four major categories of discrepancy. Specifically, the algorithm recommended higher levels of care than the clinicians in 81% of the discrepant cases.

Certain reasons for this restrictiveness have already been identified: the ease with which the algorithm is "triggered" to recommend higher levels by single items, when additional items would have provided fuller coverage of the PPC constructs or dimensions; insufficient use of contextual and balanced information to inform LOC recommendations; lack of sufficient differentiation between measures of dimensions 5 and 6; and reasoned departures by clinicians from certain PPC rules for combining dimensional scores.

Some of the revisions to the original ASAM PPC have made the criteria potentially less restrictive. PPC-2 formulated more stringent criteria for Level IV detoxification and added criteria for detoxification at Levels I, II and III. Thresholds for blood pressure and pulse were no longer included as detoxification criteria, and the thresholds for triggering Level IV have been increased considerably. The ASI Medical Composite, the leading source of discrepancies for the ALG LOC=IV cases, should be dropped by the algorithm as a measure of dimension 2, Bio-medical Complications. The algorithm should not rely heavily on patient self-reports of medical problems, but rather should use actual physical examination or testing. Since patient reports might reflect patient discomfort more than medical severity, the clinicians viewed self-reports as insufficiently valid for triggering Level IV detoxification or treatment. They saw the need for hospitalization as a medical judgment for which patient testimony is important but not determinative.

Dimension 3, Emotional/Behavioral Complications, may still route some applicants unnecessarily to Level IV. A revised algorithm should improve the measurement of this dimension by utilizing more items and allowing for gradation of responses. Note that this study found that applicants with apparently severe problems on dimension 3 were often able to complete Level III treatment, by our observation, no less often than other patients.

The ASAM PPC-2R apparently expands the range of applicants appropriate for Level I outpatient services and introduces more restrictions for Level III.7 care [medically-monitored intensive inpatient services], which should be reflected in the revised algorithm.[5] However, the pervasive tendency observed in this study for the algorithm to produce more restrictive recommendations than standard clinical assessment may well persist, even if decreased, because the differences in criteria among the new placement sub-levels tend to be subtle, many of the sub-levels are not all available in particular communities, and there remain a multitude of individual algorithm items which, if misinterpreted because of their inherent difficulty or vagueness, can "trigger" a level of care higher than clinically warranted. For instance, interviewers will still be required to try to predict patient behavior under various contingencies, such as this question from the original algorithm that alone accounted for multiple Level IV designations: Is the patient "likely to exacerbate behavioral/emotional/psychiatric problems if (he/she) continues to use drugs or alcohol?"

A specific problem with the wording of the ASAM PPC and resultant algorithm items is that applicants for treatment are assumed to be currently drinking or using drugs. Yet, some applicants for treatment may have just completed a detoxification or another treatment. For these, some key questions may yield misleading responses; e.g., a person who completed a five-day inpatient detoxification three or fewer days ago, drank some alcohol again since detoxification, and drank on at least 15 days of the last 30, would be classified by the proposed revised algorithm as an "imminent withdrawal" case.

Note that the analysis of Level IV cases presented here does not imply that ALG LOC = IV recommendations are always or usually clinically unjustified. There were many applicants for treatment during the study period who were screened by the medical staff and directed to hospital detoxification; if the PPC algorithm had been applied to these applicants, presumably it would have yielded Level IV recommendations consistent with the standard medical assessment.

Overlap Between Dimensions 5 and 6: The issue of partial overlap between dimensions 5 and 6 came into sharp focus for those cases where the algorithm recommended inpatient rehabilitation (Level III) but the clinicians recommended intensive outpatient (Level II) treatment. Whereas the algorithm assigned the same score of "III" to both dimensions in 72% of these 29 discrepant cases, the clinicians assigned the same but lower dimensional score of "II" for 65% of the cases. No other pair of dimensions exhibited a similar pattern among these 29 cases for either the algorithm or the clinician assessment. Such data suggest that both the algorithm and the clinicians encountered difficulty in differentiating the dimensions, although not necessarily for the same reasons.

For the algorithm, the heavy dependence on items from Section E of the RAATE (Social/Family Environmental Status) for both dimensions and the use of one particular RAATE item (E-5) in determining scores on the two dimensions help explain the overlap. A revised algorithm could introduce greater differentiation into the set of measures used for these two dimensions. The study's clinicians advocated greater use of ASI items. For example, in the Family/Social Supports section, the ASI includes an item asking whether the people living with the patient are using substances, and an item which categorizes the patient's living environment (controlled environment, no stable circumstances, etc.).

Further, the clinicians reported that conceptual overlap between the two dimensions made it difficult for them to rate the dimensions independently, and it is possibly difficult for the algorithm to distinguish these as well. Both dimensions, according to the clinicians, address an interaction between the patient's environment and the patient's ability to cope and/or vulnerability to their environment. Thus, they both assess relapse potential, but in different ways. Dimension 5 technically addresses only relapse potential; Dimension 6 addresses the external environment as a gauge of what patients will face in their efforts to address addiction/recovery. The contrast is between inner vulnerability (Dimension 5) and outer context (Dimension 6). The two realities of inner and outer interact, hence the apparent dimensional overlap observed for both the clinicians and the algorithm. Such clarifications could help revisions to the ASAM PPC improve its validity.

The issue of dimensional overlap is partially addressed in PPC-2R, which adds the restriction that Level III 7 requires one of the two dimensional scores of "III" to be drawn from the first three dimensions. The new requirement prevents possibly overlapping scores of "III" on both dimensions 5 and 6 from qualifying a patient for this type of inpatient treatment.

In summary, in order for the ASAM PPC and its associated algorithm to be embraced by treatment programs generally, the observed differences between recommended levels of care derived from the algorithm and standard clinical assessment should be resolved. This is critical because the algorithm usually recommends more intense, and thus more expensive, levels of care. The study cannot definitively conclude which placement recommendation is "right," but does identify specific sources of disagreement that require closer examination and discussion.

Study Limitations. The algorithm's software utilized the original ASAM Criteria (PPC-1), whereas a later edition (PPC-2R) is now available, though a revised algorithm is not yet finalized. However, this progress does not render the study's findings obsolete. The new version of the PPC differentiates among sub-levels of care but does not change the four primary levels or the basic decision-making structure and rules. The types of discrepancies encountered here between standard clinical assessment and the algorithm would likely appear in a similar test of PPC-2R, though hopefully with fewer discrepancies overall. Development of the ASAM Criteria is viewed as a continuing enterprise intended to be informed by new research; thus these results will be considered as part of a future revision.[5]

Further, this was a single-site study. Thus, it is important to recognize that the "standard" clinical assessment conducted by this program may not be representative of all clinical assessments, and that level of care judgments made by these clinicians would not necessarily be similar in other settings. In addition to limited generalizability, a single site has only a limited number of treatment programs and can, as indicated, fail to represent all levels of care. The additional programmatic differentiation in PPC-2R points to the need for multi-site studies at multi-modality programs to test the ASAM Criteria and its associated algorithm.

REFERENCES

1. Morey L. Patient placement criteria: Linking typologies to managed care. Alc Health & Rsh Wld. 1996;20(1):36-44.

2. Hoffmann N, Halikas J, Mee-Lee D, Weedman R. American Society of Addiction Medicine–Patient placement criteria for the treatment of psychoactive substance use disorders. Chevy Chase, MD: American Society of Addiction Medicine, Inc., 1991.

3. American Society of Addiction Medicine. The ASAM patient placement criteria for the treatment of substance-related disorders. Second ed. Chevy Chase, MD: American Society of Addiction Medicine, Inc., 1996.

4. Gregoire TK. Factors associated with level of care assignment in substance abuse treatment. J Sub Abuse Treat. 2000;18:241-248.

5. Mee-Lee D, Shulman GD, Fishman M et al., eds. ASAM patient placement criteria for the treatment of substance-related disorders, Second ed-Revised (ASAM PPC-2R). Chevy Chase, MD: American Society of Addiction Medicine, Inc., 2001.

6. Gastfriend DR, McLellan AT. Treatment matching theoretic basis and practical implications. Med Clin North Am. 1997;81(4):945-966.

7. Turner WM, Turner KH, Reif S et al. Feasibility of multidimensional substance abuse treatment matching: Automating the ASAM patient placement criteria. Drug Al Depend. 1999;55:35-43.

Predictive Validity
of the ASAM Patient Placement Criteria
for Hospital Utilization

Estee Sharon, PsyD
Chris Krebs, MA
Winston Turner, PhD
Nitigna Desai, MD
Gregory Binus, MD
Walter Penk, PhD
David R. Gastfriend, MD

SUMMARY. We tested the validity of the ASAM Patient Placement Criteria (PPC) using the first complete and reliable computerized imple-

Estee Sharon is affiliated with the Addiction Research Program, Department of Psychiatry, Massachusetts General Hospital and Harvard Medical School, Boston, MA, and the Edith Nourse Rogers Memorial Veterans Hospital, Bedford, MA.

Chris Krebs, Nitigna Desai, Gregory Binus, and Walter Penk are affiliated with the Edith Nourse Rogers Memorial Veterans Hospital, Bedford, MA.

Winston Turner and David R. Gastfriend are affiliated with the Addiction Research Program, Department of Psychiatry, Massachusetts General Hospital and Harvard Medical School, Boston, MA.

Address correspondence to: David R. Gastfriend, MD, Director, Addiction Research Program, Massachusetts General Hospital, 388 Commonwealth Avenue, Lower Level, Boston, MA 02115 (E-mail: DGastfriend@Partners.org).

Supported by Grants # R01-DA08781 and K24-DA00427 to Dr. Gastfriend from the National Institute on Drug Abuse.

[Haworth co-indexing entry note]: "Predictive Validity of the ASAM Patient Placement Criteria for Hospital Utilization." Sharon, Estee et al. Co-published simultaneously in *Journal of Addictive Diseases* (The Haworth Medical Press, an imprint of The Haworth Press, Inc.) Vol. 22, Supplement No. 1, 2003, pp. 79-93; and: *Addiction Treatment Matching: Research Foundations of the American Society of Addiction Medicine (ASAM) Criteria* (ed: David R. Gastfriend) The Haworth Medical Press, an imprint of The Haworth Press, Inc., 2003, pp. 79-93. Single or multiple copies of this article are available for a fee from The Haworth Document Delivery Service [1-800-HAWORTH, 9:00 a.m. - 5:00 p.m. (EST). E-mail address: docdelivery@haworthpress.com].

mentation of these criteria. Adult U.S. veterans (N = 95) seeking substance abuse treatment were blindly assessed for level of care need according to the PPC but were naturalistically assigned by counselors to residential rehabilitation (Level III) without knowledge of the PPC recommendation. Analyses compared subjects across three levels of recommended care, based on the algorithm, for utilization outcomes of VA hospital admissions and bed days of care. Subjects who were mismatched to lesser level of care than recommended utilized nearly twice as many hospital bed-days over the subsequent year (F (2;92) = 3.88; p < .05); this was unrelated to differential pre-assessment chronicity. The computerized algorithm is a promising new tool for facilitating field trials of the validity of the ASAM Criteria. A comprehensive implementation is an important methodologic requirement. These preliminary results support predictive validity for the ASAM Criteria, in that mismatching may be associated with excessive hospital utilization. *[Article copies available for a fee from The Haworth Document Delivery Service: 1-800-HAWORTH. E-mail address: <docdelivery@haworthpress.com> Website: <http://www. HaworthPress.com> © 2003 by The Haworth Press, Inc. All rights reserved.]*

KEYWORDS. ASAM level of care, substance abuse treatment outcome, utilization, predictive validity, readmission

BACKGROUND

Chronic, multifactorial diseases such as the psychoactive substance use disorders pose challenges for optimizing treatment planning in large, resource-limited systems.[1,2] Standardized, multidimensional treatment matching might provide objectivity and offer system planners opportunities to improve clinical service delivery,[3,4] but studies have been few,[5,6] and technically difficult.[7] One effort to achieve this goal is the Patient Placement Criteria (PPC) published originally in 1991 by the American Society of Addiction Medicine (ASAM).[8] These non-proprietary criteria raised considerable interest among providers, and some degree of adoption by managed care, state, and federal entities.[6] In 1997, the U.S. Veterans Administration recommended the ASAM Criteria for use in its 171 hospitals nationwide. The ASAM Criteria have also been approved by over 20 states, by one of the largest U.S. managed behavioral healthcare organizations and for worldwide use by the U.S. Department of Defense. An important concern was raised, however,[9] that these consensus guidelines have undergone no process of field trial testing and two predecessors had undergone little or no testing as well: the Criteria of the National Association of Addiction Treatment Providers and the Cleveland Criteria.[10] McKay et al. retrospectively tested a portion of the ASAM Criteria, but this incomplete implementation did not yield clear evidence of validity.[11] The Boston Target Cities Project used a version of the ASAM Criteria that was modified with ASAM's approval by the Massachusetts Bureau of Substance Abuse Services in a large, urban, public population.[12] In this project, three regional central intake units used standardized assessment with a one-page table summarizing a modified version of the ASAM Criteria. Compared to direct self-referred admission to treatment programs, patients who were referred via the centralized intake centers were significantly more likely to transition to longitudinal treatment within 30 days (i.e., outpatient care following detoxification) (odds ratio = 1.55, p < .005) and showed reduced short-term inpatient substance abuse utilization. The group that received ASAM-assisted treatment planning was significantly less likely to return for detoxification within 90 days (odds ratio = .57; p < .005).[13] This project, however, also did not use a complete implementation of the ASAM Criteria and did not evaluate the readmission or utilization rates of matched vs. mismatched cohorts.[14]

In order to examine the validity of a complete implementation of the ASAM Criteria, a naturalistic study of the ASAM Criteria was conducted at a Veterans Administration hospital in suburban, eastern Massachusetts. This facility offered substance dependent veterans residential rehabilitation, in a combination intensive outpatient (i.e., day treatment) program with supervised residential overnight care. Although the U.S. Veterans Administration had previously required nationwide adoption of the InterQual standards for utilization management, the investigators sought to study the ASAM Criteria for their specialized focus on substance use disorders, as this need has been raised repeatedly for the VA system due to rising cost concerns.[15,16] Given criticism of the ASAM Criteria from at least one managed care organization[9] and the fact that no prior study had employed a complete implementation of the ASAM Criteria, the investigators chose to conduct a preliminary field trial using a comprehensive, computerized algorithm developed for the NIDA-funded ASAM Criteria Validity Study[17] using the ASAM PPC first edition (PPC-1) as a prototype for this and subsequent editions.[18,19] In that study, the algorithm distinguished numerous cross-sectional group differences between patients assessed as requiring three different treatment settings: Level II (intensive outpatient care, e.g., day treatment), Level III (medically monitored inpatient care, e.g., non-hospital residential rehabilitation) and Level IV (medically managed inpatient care, e.g., hospital rehabilitation). Also, this algorithm was the first implementation of the ASAM PPC for which inter-rater reliability for the Level of Care determination was established, with an overall intraclass correlation coefficient of .77.[20]

The principal hypothesis of this study was that if the ASAM PPC are valid, patients assigned to a lower level of care (LOC) than recommended by the Criteria should be expected to experience worse outcomes than patients who receive care that is matched according to the recommended level or more intensive than recommended. Alterman et al. previously found a relationship between psychiatric needs and services received in veterans with substance dependence, and a greater amount of services was associated with better outcome.[21] Ideally, a test of the treatment matching hypothesis requires the availability of all LOCs and randomization across all levels. For this preliminary trial the investigators designed a prospective, naturalistic study of patients whose needs qualified them for either of the three most intensive LOC but who were all assigned to only one available treatment: non-hospital, residential care, or Level III. This LOC is of interest because of the VA system's reduction in hospital level care.[15] Therefore, the hypothesis would be supported if patients who qualified for Level IV according to the ASAM PPC but were mismatched to Level III were found to have worse outcomes than those who both required Level III and received it, or required only Level II, and received more than adequate care, i.e., Level III. Outcome research in substance use disorders may examine a variety of measures, but two ecologically relevant measures are subsequent readmission and length of stay (LOS). This study tested outcomes in terms of re-admissions and LOS because these variables are of particular interest to large, multi-facility systems responsible for optimizing resources across geographic regions.[15,16]

METHODS

This study was conducted between September 1995 and April 1997. The study sample consists of a consecutive series of veterans who attended treatment for a primary substance-related diagnosis. The inclusion/exclusion criteria included English language capability, and capacity and willingness to undergo the naturalistic interview and provide voluntary consent. The ASAM Criteria computerized interviews were administered within 72 hours after the veterans' entry to treatment. The computerized interview, with a mean duration of administration of under 60 minutes, implemented all six ASAM dimensions, prompting the interviewer, question-by-question, to ask the patient and then interpret responses as trained, with an established inter-rater reliability of .77 (intraclass coefficient), using item response formats according to the algorithm's 'feeder instruments' such as the Addiction Severity Index, and the Clinical Institute Withdrawal Assessment (for details of the computerized interview, see Baker and Gastfriend, this volume; also, Turner et al. 1999). Each subject was qualified for a distinct ASAM LOC, but the actual treatment assignment was based on a naturalistic combination of patient preference, clinical judgment, and availability of services without the benefit of the ASAM PPC recommendation. Subjects, treatment staff, and raters were all kept blind as to the results of the computerized algorithm assessment of ASAM PPC-1 LOC.

All subjects were admitted to the treatment program based on the following admission criteria: no active use of controlled substances, no active suicidal behavior or uncontrolled frank psychosis, and no prior admission into the program within the past three months. Over the period of study, the program underwent some transition, however, LOS was individualized and averaged approximately 14 days throughout.

Outcome determinations were obtained by examining the veterans' central files in Austin, Texas. Data were extracted pertaining to nationwide VA admissions to medical, psychiatric, and substance use disorder inpatient units throughout FY 1995 to 1997 (October 1994-September 1997). The variables that measure utilization of inpatient services include number of re-admissions and aggregate LOS (i.e., total bed-days of care). The association between treatment match and inpatient service utilization was examined by employing the following procedure. The ASAM evaluation date was used to split the data into utilization of inpatient services before and after that date, however, the index admission total bed-days of care was removed from the pre- and post-index admission analysis. The ASAM PPC evaluation was conducted at different times, generating a different range of before/after months for each subject. The number of months between October 1, 1994 and the ASAM PPC evaluation date provides the total number of months before ASAM PPC evaluation. The number of months between the ASAM PPC interview date and September 30, 1997 provides the total number of months after the ASAM PPC evaluation.

Two time windows of observation were calculated from the available dataset: The mean number of admissions before vs. after the index ASAM evaluation was obtained by dividing each subject's total admissions before the ASAM interview and after, by the unique number of months that had passed before and after the interview. The same procedure was used for obtaining the average number of bed-days of care before/after the ASAM PPC interview. To facilitate the interpretation of the findings, a common time denominator was used to standardize the means by annualizing them (i.e., multiplying by 12 months).

The subjects were grouped according to the treatment-match variable. All subjects were treated in the ASAM equivalent of Level III (a combination of intensive outpatient with a staff-monitored short-term residential unit, a LOC that was implied in PPC-1 and has since been specifically endorsed in the PPC-2R). Those qualified by the ASAM PPC for Level IV form the mismatch-to-lower LOC group; those qualified for Level III are the treatment-match group. Those qualified for Level II form the mismatch-to-higher LOC group. Determination of the effects of matching vs. mis-matching was performed across all three LOC using analysis of variance, followed by the post-hoc Scheffe test to determine the significance of differences between pairs of levels.

RESULTS

Sample Characteristics

All subjects were U.S. veterans (N = 95), 99% of whom were male with a racial distribution of 82% Caucasian, 16% African-American, and 2% other minorities (American Indian, Alaskan, Hispanic). The mean age of the sample was 44.9 years (± 9.2 years SD), and the educational mean was 12.4 years (± 2 years SD). Most subjects were either divorced/separated (54%) or never married (34%). One-third of the sample was homeless, and the remaining two-thirds lived alone (32%) or with family or friends (34%). In terms of work status, 33% reported unemployment at the time of the ASAM PPC evaluation, 15% considered themselves students or retired, and 52% were employed at least part-time. Subjects reported being paid for work for 5.7 (± 8.9 SD) days in the previous month, with a net income during the past month of $288 (± $637 SD). Demographic characteristics were tested across the three ASAM PPC groups and no significant differences were found for age, gender, years of education, number of days paid in last month, or net income during past month.

Clinical Status

The most frequently reported substance of choice category for this group was alcohol only (49%), with 27% reporting alcohol with drugs, and 16% reporting drugs only. During the month prior to admission, subjects reported means of 12.3 ($\pm$ 11.0 SD) days of alcohol use, 3.7 ($\pm$ 7.7 SD) days of cocaine use, 2.1 ($\pm$ 5.7 SD) days of cannabis use, and 1.8 ($\pm$ 5.9 SD) days of heroin use. Subjects are characterized according to composite scores on all Addiction Severity Index (ASI) dimensions in Table 1.[22] The scores on alcohol and opiate withdrawal ratings were low, reflecting the post-detoxification status of this cohort (CIWA-Ar, Clinical Institute Withdrawal Assessment-Revised: 1.73 $\pm$ 3.02;[23] CINA, Clinical Institute Narcotic Assessment: .72 $\pm$ 1.29[24]). Delirium and dementia were also not present according to scores on the Mini-Mental Status test (MMS: 29.1 $\pm$ 1.25).[25]

Distribution of Sample According to the ASAM Criteria

Using the computerized algorithm to determine the LOC recommended by the ASAM PPC, 28% of the veteran sample qualified for

TABLE 1. Mean Baseline Clinical Status Differences of Patients by Algorithm-Recommended ASAM Level of Care

Measure	Level-II (N = 27)	Level-III (N = 45)	Level-IV (N = 23)
ASI Composite Score			
Medical	0.11 (.20)	0.18 (.26)	0.48 (.42)**
Employment	0.66 (.25)	0.72 (.26)	0.77 (.27)
Alcohol	0.50 (.29)	0.52 (.30)	0.50 (.31)
Drug	0.14 (.17)	0.12 (.13)	0.12 (.12)
Legal	0.05 (.13)	0.07 (.15)	0.02 (0.07)
Family	0.11 (.17)	0.07 (.14)	0.09 (.17)
Psychiatric	0.17 (.21)	0.25 (.24)	0.40 (.28)**
CIWA-Ar Total	0.74 (1.43)	1.64 (3.13)	3.04 (3.75)*
CINA Total	0.26 (.59)	0.82 (1.34)	1.04 (1.66)
Mini-Mental Status	29.54 (.86)	28.91 (1.38)	29.04 (1.30)

*P < .05, **P < .01, ***P < .001; Scheffe results for significant comparisons: ASI Medical: Level IV > Level II or III, p < .01; ASI Psychiatric: Level IV > II, p < .01; CIWA Total: Level IV > II, p < .05.

Level II, 47% for Level III, and 25% for Level IV (Figure 1). Since all subjects received residential rehab (Level III), only the 47% recommended for Level III by the algorithm were considered correctly matched. Conversely, 53% of subjects were mismatched to treatment: 28% received a more intensive and restrictive treatment and 25% received a less intensive treatment than would be recommended by the ASAM PPC. Therefore, this distribution of subjects offered a naturalistic opportunity to detect differential utilization rates across match/mismatch conditions.

Four measures were examined to determine if subjects sorted by the ASAM PPC algorithm into the three LOC groups were clinically distinct: the ASI, the CIWA-Ar and CINA withdrawal measures, and MMS scores (Table 1). Some of the question items used in the computerized assessment are drawn from the measures used in this analysis of concurrent validity, however overlap is minimized because full measure scale scores do not participate in the PPC algorithm. The algorithm's groupings for Levels II, III, and IV yielded progressively more severe scores on ASI medical and psychiatric composite scores as well as the CIWA alcohol withdrawal scale and these were significant at $p \leq .05$, although the CIWA differences were not clinically meaningful.

FIGURE 1. Distribution of Veterans by Qualified Level of Care

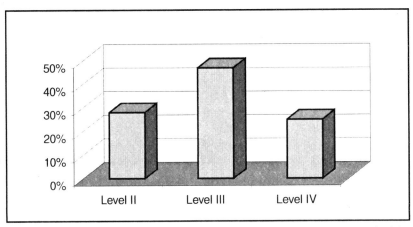

Percent of sample (N = 95) calculated by the computerized algorithm to require each of three levels of care, according to the ASAM Patient Placement Criteria.

Utilization Outcomes Across Match/Mismatch Conditions

Overall, during the three-year service utilization review period, the mean number of admissions increases with ASAM Level of Care from 3.85 for Level II to 4.11 for Level III to 5.65 for Level IV, although these differences are not significantly different. The mean bed-days of care per year shows substantial differences among subjects; veterans whom the ASAM PPC qualified for Level IV (i.e., more severe substance dependence patients) had nearly double the average number of bed-days of care than subjects who were qualified for Level II or Level III. This finding was significant (p < .05) and post-hoc testing indicated that the group which the ASAM Criteria found to need hospital care at the index admission experienced significantly more bed-days than each of the other groups: the one that was treatment-matched and the one that was mismatched-to-higher LOC.

Further analysis was undertaken to explore whether these differential outcomes were due to a chronicity effect only or due to the impact of treatment mismatching. In the former case, the disease chronicity (i.e., pre-assessment history of frequent hospital utilization) of the Level IV group might conceivably have been greater than the other groups, resulting in more bed-days, regardless of the actual treatment match status. Differential outcomes based on a chronicity effect would be of interest and might even support a form of validity for the ASAM PPC, i.e., as a disease staging system. However, if the differential outcomes were found to be strongly associated with a chronicity effect alone, this would not support the validity of the ASAM PPC as predicting which patient should be matched to which treatment. To distinguish between chronicity vs. matching effects, therefore, the outcome variables were examined both before and after the index treatment.

The time window of study observation using this dataset was as follows: The mean number of months before the ASAM PPC interview was 24.3 (± 5) months with a range of 14.8 to 31.1 months. The mean number of months after the ASAM evaluation was 13.1 (± 5.1) months with a range between 5.1 and 24.5 months. ANOVA comparisons across the three groups yielded no significant differences in the observation windows of pre-index or post-index period. The distributions of the annualized average utilization variables for each of the treatment-match levels were then examined. Two subjects were identified as outliers and were therefore excluded from further analyses due to data falling in a range beyond 3 standard deviations from the mean. One of these subjects belonged to the treatment-match group and the other to the mismatch-to-lower-LOC group. Therefore, the final sample size for this analysis is 93 veterans.

Table 2 displays service utilization means for periods before and after the ASAM interview by treatment-match groups. Subjects in the distinct treatment-match groups did not yield significantly different re-admission rates for periods before the ASAM evaluation date and after that date. Treatment-match groups also did not differ in the bed-days of care used before the ASAM PPC evaluation date. However, subjects mismatched to lower LOC used approximately three times more bed-days of care than those matched to treatment or those mismatched to higher LOC, and this was significant ($p = .03$) only for the period after the index mismatched placement (i.e., after ASAM PPC evaluation date).

DISCUSSION

These findings, while preliminary, provide the first rigorous utilization evidence that the ASAM Criteria may offer predictive validity for treatment matching of substance dependent patients to levels of care. These outcomes show significantly and substantially increased mean annualized bed-days of care for patients who are mismatched to treatments that are less intensive than what is recommended by the ASAM Criteria. This finding addresses, in part, the question raised by an earlier study of 85,000 veterans that found progressive increases in utilization over time by alcoholics and questioned whether focused treatments would achieve lower utilization.[16] It agrees with and extends the finding by Chen et al. that substantial numbers of veterans with substance dependence show multiple dimensions of need for residential or inpatient care.[15] It also agrees with the finding reported by Magura et al.[26] in a larger New York City naturalistic study that found predictive validity for the same ASAM PPC-1 computerized algorithm using a clinical outcome measure, alcohol consumption frequency at 90 days.

Interpretation of this study must take into account issues of naturalistic vs. randomized control. There are certain advantages to the naturalistic approach, which is legitimized in part by the early stage of the field of criteria testing and the lack of prior studies of a full implementation. The naturalistic approach also has the benefit of permitting a study across three levels of care, which would be difficult if not impossible to perform in a randomized design because of ethical reasons that include

TABLE 2. Service utilization for periods before and after ASAM assessment by treatment-match status

ASAM PPC match status	Annualized average admissions before ASAM interview	Annualized average admissions after ASAM interview	Annualized average bed-days of care before ASAM interview	Annualized average bed-days of care after ASAM interview
Level II (e.g., day treatment) (Mismatch-to-higher Level of Care) [N = 27]	1.16 (2.14)	1.11 (2.22)	12.17 (21.16)	9.8 (18.24)
Level III (e.g., residential) (Treatment-match) [N = 44]	1.27 (1.44)	1.38 (2.24)	16.80 (28.06)	11.43 (28.12)
Level IV (e.g., hospital) (Mismatch-to-lower Level of Care) [N = 22]	1.83 (2.03)	1.68 (1.83)	26.45 (32.76)	33.90 (59.09)
Statistical Analysis:				
one-way-ANOVA	$F_{(2;90)} = 0.95$ p = .39 n.s.	$F_{(2;90)} = 0.43$ p = .65 n.s.	$F_{(2;90)} = 1.68$ p = .19 n.s.	$F_{(2;90)} = 3.49$ **p = .03**
Post-hoc Scheffe test	not applicable	not applicable	not applicable	Level-IV > Level-II or Level-III; **p < .05**

medical safety. For example, in the ASAM Criteria Validity Study, the randomized control design requires that patients qualified for Level IV hospital care must be excluded, since a mismatched randomization to Level II day treatment might be medically or psychiatrically unsafe. Another benefit of the naturalistic design is that it is ecologically relevant, studying a sample that more closely resembles the general substance-dependent population than a sample that has been constrained by the exclusion criteria of a randomized trial.

Given questions raised by federal reviewers[3,6] and managed care[9] about the validity of the ASAM PPC, rigorous validity tests are needed. The approach of this study highlights the crucial importance of full implementation of the PPC. The advantages of this design over prior studies include a strict implementation of the ASAM PPC, with established reliability, a functional outcome that integrates substance abuse, psychiatric, medical and cost variables, and an adequate duration of follow-up. This study used a mean duration of follow-up of over one year. The primary outcome variable was available via a nationwide, centralized database to capture all VA hospital admissions and bed-days that might be utilized by this veteran population.

Limitations of this design affect the replicability of the results in larger samples and their interpretation. Constraints on the study's conclusions are necessary due to its small sample size and naturalistic method. The possibility also exists that some veterans obtained admissions outside of VA facilities, a potential source of data loss that limits the use of readmission as a proxy for clinical outcome.[27] Given this possible data loss and the limited number of subjects, it is promising that significant results support the validity of the PPC. Further analysis would be needed to determine if lower-than-recommended level of care resulted in differentially increased admission to psychiatric or medical beds, implying ineffective attention was paid to psychiatric and medical comorbidity. It should be noted, however, that hospital utilization rate is a volatile outcome measure that may be vulnerable to variability from individual case differences and local admission and discharge criteria. Also, subsequent medical admissions could reflect appropriately increased utilization following addiction stabilization and may not necessarily represent an adverse outcome. For this reason, future studies need to measure these outcomes in substantial VA and non-VA samples.

It is important to recognize the limitations of not employing randomization and not offering a complete range of naturalistic treatment assignments. This study lacked a cohort of subjects who required and also received Level IV hospital care. It also lacked a cohort that required

Level II day treatment and received it. It is, therefore, not entirely possible to determine whether higher rates of utilization are actually attributable to mismatching or whether the ASAM PPC only predict cohort chronicity. Without the Level IV matched group, in particular, the study was unable to conclusively test whether a differential treatment response results from Level IV matching or whether Level IV patients always have worse outcomes than Level III or II patients–both when matched or mismatched. The retrospective approach employed here to detect any significant prior group differences failed to find a significant cohort effect, however, this method is not definitive and a larger sample may have yielded support for the cohort effect as well.

Despite these limitations, the design is an efficient approach to determining preliminary validity for the ASAM PPC as a system of characterizing multidimensional substance abuse problems. Future studies need to assess subjects across multiple sites to account for local variability in treatment access and utilization. Randomized, controlled designs in larger samples with distinct proximal and distal timeframes such as the NIDA-funded ASAM Criteria Validity Study remain necessary to fully test the validity of such criteria. Studies also need to examine the predictive validity of the algorithm for clinical outcomes, such as substance use, social, vocational, legal, and psychiatric severity and general health function, all of which are variables being analyzed in the ASAM Criteria Validity Study underway by our group.

REFERENCES

1. McLellan A, Woody G, Metzger D, et al. Evaluating the effectiveness of treatments for substance use disorders: Appropriate comparisons. Milbank Quart. 1996; 74(1):51-85.

2. Gastfriend DR, McLellan AT. Treatment matching: Theoretic basis and practical implications. Med Clin N Amer. 1997;81(4):945-966.

3. Morey L. Patient placement criteria Linking typologies to managed care. Alc Health & Rsh Wld. 1996;20(1):36-44.

4. Gastfriend D. Patient Placement Criteria. In: Galanter M, Kleber HD, eds. Textbook of Substance Abuse Treatment. Second Ed. Washington: The American Psychiatric Press, 1999:121-127.

5. Institute of Medicine. Broadening the Base of Treatment for Alcohol Problems: A Report of a Study by a Committee of the Institute of Medicine, Division of Mental Health and Behavioral Medicine. Washington, DC: National Academy Press, 1990.

6. Center for Substance Abuse Treatment. The Role and Current Status of Patient Placement Criteria in the Treatment of Substance Use Disorders. Treatment Improve-

ment Protocol (TIP). Rockville, MD: Substance Abuse and Mental Health Services Administration, 1995.

7. McLellan AT, Grissom GR, Zanis D, et al. Problem-service 'Matching' in addiction treatment: A prospective study in 4 programs. Arch Gen Psychiatry. 1997; 54(8):730-735.

8. Hoffmann N, Halikas J, Mee-Lee D, Weedman R. American Society of Addiction Medicine–Patient Placement Criteria for the treatment of psychoactive substance use disorders. 1st ed. Washington, DC: ASAM, 1991.

9. Book J, Harbim H, Marques C, et al. The ASAM's and Green Spring's alcohol and drug detoxification and rehabilitation criteria for utilization review. Am J Addiction. 1995; 4(3):187-197.

10. Hoffmann N, Halikas J, Mee-Lee D. The Cleveland Admission, Discharge and Transfer Criteria: Model for Chemical Dependency Treatment Programs. Cleveland, OH: Northern Ohio Chemical Dependency Treatment Consortium, 1987.

11. McKay JR, Cacciola JS, McLellan AT, et al. An initial evaluation of the psychosocial dimensions of the American Society of Addiction Medicine criteria for inpatient vs. intensive outpatient substance abuse rehabilitation. J Stud Alcohol. 1997;58(5):239-252.

12. Plough A, Shirley L, Zaremba N, et al. CSAT target cities demonstration final evaluation report: Boston Office for Treatment Improvement, 1996.

13. Shwartz M, Gastfriend DR, Mulvey K, et al. The Boston Target Cities Program: Overview and evaluation results. J Psychoactive Drugs. 1999;31(3):265-272.

14. Gastfriend DR, Lu S, Sharon E. Substance use & misuse. Marcel Dekker, Inc. 2000:2191-2213.

15. Chen S, Wagner TH, Barnett PG. The effect of reforms on spending for veterans' substance abuse treatment. Health Affairs. 2001;20(4):169-175.

16. Booth BM, Blow FC, Cook CA, et al. Relationship between inpatient alcoholism treatment and longitudinal changes in health care utilization. J Stud Alcohol. 1997; 58(6):625-637.

17. Turner WM, Turner KH, Reif S, et al. Feasibility of multidimensional substance abuse treatment matching: Automating the ASAM Patient Placement Criteria. Drug Alc Depend. 1999; 55:35-43.

18. American Society of Addiction Medicine. ASAM PPC-2R/ASAM Patient Placement Criteria for the Treatment of Substance-Related Disorders. Second Edition–Revised ed. Maryland: American Society of Addiction Medicine (ASAM), 2001.

19. Mee-Lee D, Shulman GD, Fishman M et al., eds. ASAM Patient Placement Criteria for the Treatment of Substance-Related Disorders, Second Edition-Revised (ASAM PPC-2R). Chevy Chase, MD: American Society of Addiction Medicine, Inc., 2001.

20. Baker SL, Gastfriend DR. Reliability of multidimensional substance abuse treatment matching: Implementing the ASAM patient placement criteria. J Addict Dis. 2003; 22(S):45-60.

21. Alterman AI, McLellan AT, Shifman RB. Do substance abuse patients with more psychopathology receive more treatment? J Nerv Ment Dis. 1993; 181:576-582.

22. McLellan A, Kushner H, Metzger M, et al. The fifth edition of the Addiction Severity Index. J Subst Abuse Treat. 1992; 9:199-213.

23. Sullivan JT, Sykora K, Schneiderman J, et al. Assessment of alcohol withdrawal: The revised Clinical Institute Withdrawal Assessment for Alcohol Scale. Br J Addict. 1989; 84:1353-1357.

24. Fudala PJ, Berkow LC, Fralich JL, Johnson RE. Use of naloxone in the assessment of opiate dependence. Life Sci. 1991; 49(24):1809-1814.

25. Folstein MF, Folstein SE, McHugh PR. "Mini-mental state." A practical method for grading the cognitive state of patients for the clinician. J Psychiatr Res. 1975;12:189-198.

26. Magura S, Staines G, Kosanke N, et al. Predictive validity of the ASAM Patient Placement Criteria: Outcomes for patients naturalistically matched and mismatched to Levels of Care. Am J Addict. 2003; 12:386-397.

27. Humphreys K, Weingardt KR. Assessing readmission to substance abuse treatment as an indicator of outcome and program performance. Psychiatr Serv. 2000; 51:1568-1569.

New Constructs and Assessments for Relapse and Continued Use Potential in the ASAM Patient Placement Criteria

David R. Gastfriend, MD
Amy Rubin, PhD
Estee Sharon, PsyD
Winston M. Turner, PhD
Raymond F. Anton, MD

Dennis M. Donovan, PhD
Terence Gorski, PhD
G. Alan Marlatt, PhD
Steven Maisto, PhD
Terry K. Schultz, MD

Gerald D. Shulman, LICSW, MA

David R. Gastfriend, Amy Rubin, and Estee Sharon are affiliated with the Addiction Research Program, Department of Psychiatry, Massachusetts General Hospital.

Winston M. Turner is Project Director, University of Maine School of Social Work.

Raymond F. Anton is affiliated with the Center for Drug and Alcohol Programs, Institute of Psychiatry, Medical University of South Carolina.

Dennis M. Donovan is affiliated with the Alcohol & Drug Abuse Institute, University of Washington.

Terence Gorski is affiliated with the CENAPS Center, Homewood, IL.

G. Alan Marlatt is affiliated with the Department of Psychology, University of Washington.

Steven Maisto is affiliated with the Department of Psychology, Syracuse University.

Terry K. Schultz is Director, Addiction Medicine, Mid-Atlantic Kaiser Permanente Medical Group, and Co-Chair, ASAM State of the Art Conference, Arlington, VA.

Gerald D. Shulman is President, Shulman & Associates, Training and Consulting in Behavioral Health, and Deputy Editor, ASAM PPC-2R, Jacksonville, FL.

Address correspondence to: David R. Gastfriend, MD, Director, Addiction Research Program, Massachusetts General Hospital, 388 Commonwealth Avenue, Lower Level, Boston, MA 02115 (E-mail: DGastfriend@Partners.org).

Supported by Grants # R01-DA08781 and K24-DA00427 to Dr. Gastfriend from the National Institute on Drug Abuse.

Based on material from the following publication and reprinted with the permission of the publisher: Mee-Lee D, Shulman GD, Fishman M, Gastfriend DR, and Griffith JH, eds. *ASAM Patient Placement Criteria for the Treatment of Substance-Related Disorders, Second Edition-Revised (ASAM PPC-2R)*. Chevy Chase, MD: American Society of Addiction Medicine, Inc., 2001.

[Haworth co-indexing entry note]: "New Constructs and Assessments for Relapse and Continued Use Potential in the ASAM Patient Placement Criteria." Gastfriend, David R. et al. Co-published simultaneously in *Journal of Addictive Diseases* (The Haworth Medical Press, an imprint of The Haworth Press, Inc.) Vol. 22, Supplement No. 1, 2003, pp. 95-111; and: *Addiction Treatment Matching: Research Foundations of the American Society of Addiction Medicine (ASAM) Criteria* (ed: David R. Gastfriend) The Haworth Medical Press, an imprint of The Haworth Press, Inc., 2003, pp. 95-111. Single or multiple copies of this article are available for a fee from The Haworth Document Delivery Service [1-800-HAWORTH, 9:00 a.m. - 5:00 p.m. (EST). E-mail address: docdelivery@haworthpress.com].

http://www.haworthpress.com/store/product.asp?sku=J069
Digital Object Identifier: 10.1300/J069v22S01_07

95

SUMMARY. One area of intensive study in recent years in addiction research is the characterization and prediction of relapse risk. Given the growing list of findings and assessment tools in this area, in preparation for the second edition, revised volume of the Patient Placement Criteria (PPC) of the American Society of Addiction Medicine (ASAM), a workgroup of the Coalition for National Criteria was assigned the task of creating a revised conceptual organization for Dimension 5: Relapse/Continued Use Potential.

The workgroup conducted a review of the previous Dimension 5 constructs and criteria, including a decision analysis of the previous Dimension 5 decision rules. Following that analysis, field data from the ASAM Criteria Validity Study at Massachusetts General Hospital and Harvard Medical School were analyzed from a large cohort of public and indigent patients in eastern Massachusetts. After determining the concurrent validity of the Dimension 5 decision rules and their limitations, the decision rules were rewritten to gain improved validity. This exercise revealed techniques that can and should be used to improve the discrimination of levels of care among all Dimensions. Finally, the workgroup expanded and refined the constructs that should comprise a revised Dimension 5. This revised list of constructs is sequential and hierarchical. It offers face validity on several levels of current basic and clinical research knowledge: behavioral pharmacology, behavioral psychology, learning theory and psychopathology.

While the Second Edition-Revised volume of the ASAM PPC (PPC-2R) does not go so far as to propose final decision rules for Dimension 5 based on these new constructs, it does recommend pilot adoption of several new assessment tools for this dimension and provides the framework incorporating those constructs and assessments in the next complete PPC edition. *[Article copies available for a fee from The Haworth Document Delivery Service: 1-800-HAWORTH. E-mail address: <docdelivery@haworthpress.com> Website: <http://www.HaworthPress.com>]*

KEYWORDS. ASAM criteria, substance abuse assessment, relapse, craving

BACKGROUND

History of Constructs and Criteria of Dimension 5: Relapse Potential

In preparation for the PPC-2R,[1] a workgroup of the Coalition for National Criteria was asked to critically review the state of the art of data on assessing and predicting relapse potential. The original 1991 ASAM Patient Placement Criteria (PPC-1) described a Dimension 5, entitled "Relapse Potential,"[2] that required an assessment of several drinking related factors, such as the risk of immediate danger, the risk of continued drinking/drug-taking behavior, the patient's understanding of the necessary skills for preventing relapse, the severity of further distress if the patient fails to engage in treatment, his/her awareness of relapse triggers, and skills for coping with cravings and controlling impulses.

In the 1996 second edition of the ASAM PPC (PPC-2),[3] Dimension 5 was expanded to include assessment of continued use potential, since many patients may not have achieved any significant abstinence yet beyond withdrawal and thus cannot meet the definition of "relapse." The PPC-2 Dimension 5 required assessment as specified below to determine which would be the most appropriate from among the following service levels:

Level 0.5–Early Intervention Services: for the patient who would need an understanding of the risks of, or skills to change, current use patterns.

Level I–Outpatient Services: for the patient who could control use or maintain abstinence while pursuing recovery goals with minimal support.

Level II–Intensive Outpatient Treatment: if the patient was experiencing intensified addiction symptoms and functional deterioration despite participating in a less intensive level of care (LOC) and despite efforts to revise the treatment plan. A distinction was made between Level II.1–Intensive Outpatient Treatment vs. Level II.5–Partial Hospitalization. The latter was reserved for the patient who had failed Level II.1 services or for whom continued drinking/drug use or impending relapse was likely and for whom less intensive treatment would be insufficient for stabilization.

Level III–Residential Services: when a patient's impending relapse or continued use would be associated with imminent danger in the absence of 24 hour structured support. This circumstance might result from an inability to cope with environmental access to substances, difficulty postponing immediate gratification or, in the event of Level III.3–Clinically Managed Medium Intensity Residential Treatment, cognitive limitations, chronicity or a high intensity of substance use. In the less structured but still residential Level III.1–Clinically Managed Low Intensity Residential Treatment, the patient understands his/her problems, but would be at risk because of an inability to apply recovery skills.

Opioid Maintenance Therapy: when an opioid dependent patient would be at risk of relapse because of any of the following three reasons: (1) physiological craving, or (2) intensification of addiction symptoms, or (3) continued high-risk behaviors with deteriorating function despite non-maintenance treatments and treatment plan adjustment efforts. Alternatively, Level OMT would be warranted simply because of high-risk of relapse due to either lack of awareness of triggers, difficulty postponing immediate gratification or resistance to treatment.

Implementation of a Reliable Dimension 5 Assessment for Research

In the MGH/Harvard ASAM Criteria Validity Study, Dimension 5 was implemented for the ASAM PPC-1 in a computerized algorithm using selected items from the Recovery Attitude and Treatment Evaluator (RAATE).[4] The items were taken from RAATE subscales A (Resistance to Treatment), B (Resistance to Continuing Care), and E (Environmental Factors Unsupportive of Recovery). These items provided a structured assessment of: the patient's need for motivating strategies, relapse risk training and planning, recovery supports, high-risk social networks, impaired social skills, inadequate recreational activities and degree of unstructured daily routine. Two published reports supported the construct and predictive validity of the RAATE subscales.[5,6] Two additional questions were needed from the Structured Clinical Interview for DSM-IV (SCID) Histrionic Personality Disorder Module to determine impulsivity.[7,8] New items were also required to determine past 90 day treatments, to elicit any pattern of increasing addiction symptoms, and to obtain the interviewer's evaluation of whether the patient is in imminent danger of relapse. Altogether, 18 question items were required to address the ASAM PPC-1 decision rules for Dimension 5. Results below from an interim analysis must be considered only preliminary until final sample size is accrued and data cleaning is completed; therefore, the empirical conclusions that follow should be considered illustrative only and not final.

Decision Rule Artifacts

The interim analysis detected multiple areas in which problems in the decision logic occurred as a result of the structure of the PPC and its implementation. In an analysis of 586 subjects from the ASAM Criteria Validity Study,[9,10] 107 subjects (18.3%) did not qualify for any level of care in Dimension 5. In other words, these were not necessarily patients at less risk than those who achieved a level of care score, but one who simply could not be directly scored into a level of care according to the explicit decision rules.

Another artifact of the decision logic is that nearly one-third of subjects qualified for two or more LOCs, simultaneously. Overall, 24.2% of subjects received LOC scores for both Level II and III. The largest cause of overlap occurred when raters endorsed the Level II criterion "difficulty postponing immediate gratification" at the same time as the Level III criterion "unable to limit or control use if alcohol or drugs are present in the environment." One solution to this apparent problem of overlap is to revise this dimension with entirely discrete, non-overlapping criteria. While psychometrically preferable, this is not as easy as it sounds. Alternatively, a "highest LOC" default rule can be employed in which patients who meet both the Level II and Level III criteria noted above are automatically considered to fulfill Level III requirements. This is implied in the ASAM PPC-1 and PPC-2 and has been specifically confirmed as the intent of the PPC by an expert review group that included authors of the PPC. Therefore, some overlap may not represent true shortcomings but rather hierarchical clinical decision-making. Nevertheless, there is a challenge in writing resolving and non-overlapping criteria and some degree of these problems appears to occur in most dimensions of the ASAM PPC-1, not just in Dimension 5. Further, this artifact is aggravated in PPC-2, by the LOC subdivisions.

Concurrent Validity of Dimension 5

In this study sample, subjects requiring either partial or residential treatment were recruited and assessed with the full Addiction Severity Index (ASI)[11] as well as the ASAM PPC-1 algorithm. The algorithm was based on a detailed analysis and comprehensive implementation of all dimensions and decision rules, using research quality structured interview questions, quantitative thresholds for each question response in support of a particular LOC, and software programming to provide research assistants with a question by question sequence for interviewing and scoring the volunteer research subjects. Subjects consisted of men and women with various substance dependencies from public sector samples in eastern Massachusetts. Using a highest LOC default rule to resolve overlapping cases, 199 (34%) met criteria for Dimension 5 Level II and 260 (44.4%) met criteria for Level III. Theoretically, if concurrent validity (i.e., agreement with different measures intended to rate similar constructs) is supported, patients rated on Dimension 5 as requiring Level III care should manifest higher ASI severity scores than patients requiring Level II. Of course, this is only true to the extent that Dimension 5 severity is consistent with the other dimensions. The nature of multi-dimensional assessment is that it is not necessarily linear. For example, someone may have high ASI severity but have good treatment readiness and engagement in recovery groups and be suited to Level II. Another patient may have lower ASI severity and even good readiness on Dimension 4 and yet severe craving in Dimension 5 and thus may need Level III. Results indicate that patients rated on Dimension 5 as requiring Level III indeed had marginally greater composite severity scores on the ASI subscales for Alcohol, Employment, Family, and Legal problems. Only ASI Drug and Psychiatric subscales failed to show this pattern. Baseline Global Assessment of Function (GAF) ratings also showed substantially worse function of 55.1 for subjects rated on Dimension 5 as requiring Level III, compared to 70.0 for those requiring Level II. This is therefore a reasonably consistent, clinically meaningful difference that supports concurrent validity.

Revising Dimension 5 to Create Discrete Thresholds

The MGH/Harvard group re-wrote the Dimension 5 decision rules using the same items but combining them in such a way as to avoid non-resolving or overlapping determinations. This required, in some decision rules, setting discrete thresholds along a continuum (i.e., using clinical consensus on a conflicting item to set a score below which L-I is supported, vs. a higher score for L-II, etc.) and, in others, using a simplified hierarchy of combination rules to replace multiple items that could be algebraically combined in more than one way. (Examples of the decision algorithm are available upon request from the first author.) This eliminated the non-resolving cases and resulted in a more balanced distribution of cases along Dimension 5: of the original 586 subjects, 27.5% were now rated as meeting Level I, 36.0% as Level II, and 36.5% as Level III.

Using these revised decision rules, preliminary results indicated that baseline Dimension 5 scores consistently grouped Level I, II, and III subjects in the expected staircase pattern of ascending ASI severity composite scores on the following subscales: Alcohol, Employment, Family, Legal, and Psychiatric. (Medical scores were also ascending but are not addressed in this analysis because medical exclusion criteria limited the range of the sample.) Also, the range of variance on each of these scales was somewhat greater with this revised method. In baseline

GAF scores, those who qualified for Level III were rated as least functional (56.2), followed by Level II (57.8), with Level I being most functional (68.0).

The revised method of scoring Dimension 5 also demonstrates some degree of near-term predictive validity. The interim sample for a baseline vs. month 1 comparison consisted of 271 subjects with complete data. Baseline categorization using the revised Dimension 5 scoring was associated with a higher month 1 ASI Alcohol composite score for Level III (.278 ± .256 S.D.), compared to Level II (.187 ± .212) vs. Level I (.180 ± .231)(range: 0-1.00, where increasing score indicates worsening severity and change in treatment overtime should show improvement, or decreasing severity score). This is a clinically meaningful difference between Level III and the outpatient levels. This pattern was similar for the comparison of month 1 ASI Drug composite severity for baseline Level III (.149 ± .112) compared to both Level II (.121 ± .109) and Level I (.126 ± .111), although the differential between these levels is not substantial. These relationships were not consistently maintained, however, at months 3 or 6 (which had smaller samples in this preliminary analysis–and it may be too much to expect such extended predictive associations from a single PPC dimension, in any case).

Further Problems and Considerations

A practical problem in these data is that scores on the ASI composite Medical Severity subscale were limited in range by the study's medical exclusion criteria. Naturalistic research is needed that will include patients who have severe medical problems. A theoretical problem is the possibility that acute medical crisis (e.g., acute pancreatitis) may temporarily decrease patients' subjective sense of relapse risk (e.g., since the desire to drink is temporarily eliminated due to severe pain), however, once medical problems subside relapse potential may dramatically increase. This may be analogous to a depressed patient who poses minimal suicide risk during the most severe neurovegetative symptoms but who, upon initiation of effective pharmacotherapy, improves rapidly to the point of becoming capable of acting on suicidal urges. A future revision will need to create decision rules to distinguish between an artificially low relapse risk due to short-term medical factors vs. other factors that represent low intrinsic relapse risk. Short-term confounds such as this may occur elsewhere. These may include incarceration, coercion and family intervention–all acute circumstances (assessed on Dimensions 4 and 6) that may change over time, releasing latent relapse risk.

Several variables are poorly assessed using current structured interview methods and, while considered important clinically, are difficult to measure reliably through conventional clinical interviewing. Two examples are the presence of acute coercive legal factors and approval seeking response bias. Both may invalidate self report of the patient's intrinsic relapse potential. Temporal factors such as pregnancy may make relapse potential difficult to assess beyond delivery.

Another concern is the mixing of constructs. A psychometrically coherent approach would isolate these initially for internal consistency, and combine them secondarily via a subsequent layer of cumulative decision rules. For example, individuals with comorbid psychiatric disorders may also suffer personality traits or mood disturbances that increase impulsivity, however, these must be distinguished from Dimension 5 problems which are specifically related to acute risks for substance use as opposed to chronic personality or general affective characteristics. The following constructs are proposed to improve the psychometric coherence of Dimension 5 in the next revision of the PPC.

PROPOSED REVISED CONSTRUCTS FOR DIMENSION 5: RELAPSE/CONTINUED USE POTENTIAL

A. Historical Pattern of Use

   1. Chronicity of Problem Use

      Since when and how long has the individual had problem use or dependence and at what level of severity? Related demographic variables include youth, early onset of problems, lacking a high school education, and never having married.

   2. Treatment or Change Response

      Has he/she managed brief or extended abstinence or reduction in the past?

B. Pharmacologic Responsivity

   3. Positive Reinforcement (pleasure, euphoria)

   4. Negative Reinforcement (withdrawal discomfort and fear)

C. External Stimuli Responsivity

    5. Reactivity to Acute Cues (trigger objects and situations)

    6. Reactivity to Chronic Stress (positive and negative stressors)

D. Cognitive and Behavioral Measures of Strengths and Weaknesses

    7. Locus of Control and Self-efficacy

        Is there an internal sense of self-determination and confidence that the individual can direct his/her own behavioral change?

    8. Coping Skills (including stimulus control, other cognitive strategies)

    9. Impulsivity (risk-taking, thrill-seeking)

    10. Passive and Passive/Aggressive Behavior

        Does the individual demonstrate active efforts to anticipate and cope with internal and external stressors, or is there a tendency to leave or assign responsibility to others?

These four domains are not inconsistent with the intent of the PPC-2 version of Dimension 5, but offer a conceptually more clear sequence of factors that contribute to relapse potential. The sequence involves the historical conditions of relapse, the acute pharmacologic response to substance(s), second order behavioral responsivity that may mediate the preceding factors, and third order personality or learned responses that may modify the preceding factors.

Constructs in Section A, Historical Pattern, may apply to use, abuse or dependence. Demographic variables such as onset of problems before age 25, never having married, lacking a high school education, and being unemployed have been found to predict continued use or relapse in a large number of studies. Clinical history variables, such as past treatment response, are good predictors of future relapse risk. Even if the patient has not previously undergone treatment, any past change efforts to reduce or cease substance use behavior will be informative. This may apply to substances other than the one that is the current primary risk for the patient. For example, it may be helpful to know if the patient who must cease drinking has previously succeeded in quitting smoking.

For Section B, the term Pharmacologic Responsivity refers to internal stimuli at the neuronal level of the brain from reinforcing substances that produce either or both positive and negative reinforcement. The operative role here is the patient's expectancy, i.e., to what extent does the patient expect pleasure or euphoria (for positive reinforcement), or withdrawal discomfort and fear of withdrawal (for negative reinforcement). Thus, negative reinforcement is not intended here to represent the acute withdrawal symptoms themselves, as those are addressed in Dimension 1–Intoxication/Withdrawal.

The constructs in section D differ from those in Dimension 3, Emotional/Behavioral Conditions. Section D constructs are behavioral traits that are specific to relapse risk, although they may not be pathologic in other contexts. This distinguishes them from Dimension 3 constructs, which are usually psychiatric (i.e., DSM-IV)[12] Axis I or II diagnoses, which generalize to many behaviors and risk situations.

It is important to recognize that relapse risk is constantly changing. Therefore, the time frame for prediction is limited. In a given patient, each of the above constructs is highly variable, so the patient requires frequent re-assessment as withdrawal subsides, a new treatment response is established, coping strengths are learned and tested, character traits grow and euphoric expectancies extinguish.

A Primary vs. Secondary Role for Relapse Potential in the Overall PPC Decision Tree

The importance of relapse potential is sufficient that the Committee seriously considered an alternate dimensional structure for the PPC: conceivably, all other dimensions could be assessed first, leaving relapse potential to be evaluated as a second-order, over-arching, integrative dimension to solve the final level of care decision based upon the pressure on relapse risk from all other sources. Ultimately, this was discarded as reductionistic. After considering these options, the Committee resolved to maintain the six-dimensional model of assessment, with Relapse Potential separate but equal to the other dimensions and concurrently considered. In keeping with this principle, the assessment of impulsivity and passivity was divided into two separate aspects: (a) general psychological pathology, delegated to Dimension 3, which should consider major character pathology with self harm potential; vs. (b) traits or coping characteristics that are specific to substance use relapse and relapse prevention. This latter construct is retained in the proposed Dimension 5.

PROSPECTS FOR RELIABLE ASSESSMENT

Most of these constructs have available some structured assessment items or sub-scales that are potentially useful aids for implementation.

Predictive relationships for individual constructs are relatively modest and methodology is very much in need of further development.[13,14] In the following list, selected measures are listed as examples, following each construct heading. This list is incomplete and may omit valuable instruments. Clinicians and programs should investigate alternatives and the Coalition invites submissions. The criteria for assessment tools should include: good psychometric properties, shared face (i.e., logical) validity for the purpose for which instrument was designed, brevity and appropriateness for administration to a wide range of substance abuse and dependence populations. Citations are provided for both instruments and relevant descriptive papers; some indicate commercial or fee-based sources that are also listed following the outline.

SUGGESTED INSTRUMENTS OR ITEM SOURCES OR ASSESSING DIMENSION 5: RELAPSE POTENTIAL

A. Historical Pattern of Use

    1. Chronicity of Problem Use

        Since when and how long has the individual had problem use or dependence and at what level of severity?[7,8,12]

        a. Structured Clinical Interview for DSM-IV (SCID)[7,8]
        b. Substance Use Disorder Diagnostic Schedule (SUDDS)[15,16]

    2. Treatment or Change Response

        Has he/she managed brief or extended abstinence or reduction in the past?

        Measures addressing both A.1. and A.2.:

        a. Addiction Severity Index Alcohol and Drug Severity Scales (ASI)[11,17]
        b. Form 90[18]
        c. Drinker Inventory of Consequences (DrInC)[19]
        d. Inventory of Drug Use Consequences (InDUC; based on the DrInC)[19]
        e. Alcohol Dependence Scale (ADS)[20]
        f. Drug Use Questionnaire (DAST)[21]
        g. Chemical Use, Abuse and Dependence Scale (CUAD frequency/amount/duration grid)[22]

B. Pharmacologic Responsivity

  3. Positive Reinforcement

  Amount of pleasure or euphoria patient obtains or expects from substance use. Expectancies, which may be defined as the outcome(s) the individual expects from a particular behavior, have been shown to be related to substance use consumption and relapse.

  a. Alcohol Effects Questionnaire (AEFQ) Global Positive subscale and Relaxation and Tension Reduction subscale[23,24]
  b. Alcohol Expectancies Questionnaire (AEQ)[25,26]

  4. Negative Reinforcement

  Amount of discomfort or negative effects patient expects or fears from abstaining.

  a. Craving–Obsessive Compulsive Drinking Scale, e.g., item 11(OCDS)[27,28]
  b. Alcohol Dependence Scale–e.g., item 9 (ADS; a/k/a Alcohol Use Questionnaire)[20]

C. External Stimuli Responsivity

  Acute and chronic cues and stressors may include positive stressors, including vocational achievements, as well as negative stressors, e.g., social pressure situations, conflict situations and ongoing environmental challenges such as homelessness, divorce, and financial problems.

  5. Reactivity to Acute Cues

  Reaction to trigger objects and situations both in terms of strength of reaction and the ubiquitous nature of cues.

  a. Inventory of Drinking Situations and Inventory of Drug Taking Situations (available from ARF)[29,30]
  b. Situational Confidence Questionnaire (SCQ; Annis & Graham, 1988)[31]

  6. Reactivity to Chronic Stress (positive and negative stressors)

  Ability to manage ongoing environmental stressors that are not specific to substance use, such as homelessness, divorce, financial problems.

  a. Life Experiences Survey[32]

D. Cognitive and Behavioral Measures of Strengths and Weaknesses

   7. Locus of Control and Related Assessments

      Is there an internal sense of self-determination and confidence that the individual can direct his/her own behavioral change?

      a. Recovery Attitude and Treatment Evaluator–Clinical Evaluation/Research Version, Scale B Resistance to Continuing Care (RAATE-CE/R)[4-6]

      b. Drinking Related Locus of Control Scale (DRIE).[33-36] Has also been adapted for cigarette smokers[37] and cocaine abusers.[38]

   8. Coping Skills

      Including stimulus control and other cognitive strategies[39]

      a. Recovery Attitude and Treatment Evaluator–Clinical Evaluation/Research Version, Scale B Resistance to Continuing Care, and Scale E Social/Family/Environmental Status (RAATE-CE/R)[4-6]

      URICA Action & Maintenance scale score[40]

      b. Coping Behaviors Inventory (CBI)[41] and Effectiveness of Coping Behaviors Inventory (ECBI)[42]

      c. Ways of Coping[43,44]

      d. Coping Resources Inventory (CRI; available from PAR)[45]

   9. Impulsivity (risk-taking, thrill-seeking)

      Risk taking, thrill or novelty-seeking traits (rather than pathology, which is assessed in Dimension 3–Behavioral Conditions and Complications)

      a. Personality Assessment Inventory–high scores on the Stimulus Seeking scale (PAI; available from PAR)[46]

      b. Temperament & Character Inventory (TCI)[47]

  10. Passive and Passive/Aggressive Behavior

      Does the individual demonstrate active efforts to anticipate and cope with internal and external stressors, or is there a tendency to leave or assign responsibility to others?

      Traits rather than pathological conditions that belong in Dimension 3.

a. Personality Assessment Inventory–low scores on the Dominance scale indicate passivity (PAI; available from PAR)[46]

b. See also Locus of Control (DRIE, above).[33-36] External scores on any of the three subscales indicate the individual assigns causality to events outside of their control, and tends not to attempt to change situations.

c. See also Coping Skills (CRI, above)[45]. High scores on Avoidant coping scales tend to lead to passive behavior.

SOURCES

Measures listed as available from ARF (Addiction Research Foundation) may be obtained for a fee from: Centre for Addiction and Mental Health, Addiction Research Foundation Division, Marketing and Sales Services, 33 Russell Street, Toronto, Ontario, Canada M55 2S1, Telephone: 800-661-1111.

Measures listed as available from PAR (Psychological Assessment Resources) may be obtained for a fee from: Psychological Assessment Resources, Inc., P.O. Box 998, Odessa, FL 33556, Telephone: 800-331-TEST.

The ASI (Addiction Severity Index) may be obtained for a small copying fee from: Treatment Research Institute, University of Pennsylvania, One Commerce Square, Suite 1120, 2005 Market Street, Philadelphia, PA 19103, Telephone: 215-665-2880

The SCID-I/P Patient version and CV clinician version are obtained from: SCID Central, Biometrics Research Department, New York State Psychiatric Institute, 1051 Riverside Drive–Unit 60, New York, NY 10032, Telephone: 212-543-5524, <http://cpmcnet.columbia.edu/dept/scid>.

The SUDDS may be obtained for a fee from: Evince Clinical Assessments, P.O. Box 17305, Smithfield, RI 02917.

REFERENCES

1. Mee-Lee D, Shulman GD, Fishman M et al., eds. ASAM patient placement criteria for the treatment of substance-related disorders, second edition-revised (ASAM PPC-2R). Chevy Chase: American Society of Addiction Medicine, Inc., 2001.

2. Hoffmann N, Halikas J, Mee-Lee D, Weedman R: American society of addiction medicine–patient placement criteria for the treatment of psychoactive substance use disorders. Washington: ASAM, Inc., 1991.

3. American Society of Addiction Medicine. Patient placement criteria for the treatment of substance-related disorders, second edition (ASAM PPC-2). Chevy Chase: American Society of Addiction Medicine, Inc., 1996.

4. Mee-Lee D, Hoffman NG, Smith MB. Recovery attitude and treatment evaluator (RAATE) manual (2nd ed). St. Paul: CATOR/New Standards, Inc., 1992.

5. Gastfriend DR, Filstead WJ, Reif S, et al. Validity of assessing treatment readiness in patients with substance use disorders. American Journal of Addictions. 1995; 4:254-260.

6. Najavits LM, Gastfriend DR, Nakayama EY, et al. A measure of readiness for substance abuse treatment: psychometric properties of the RAATE research interview. American Journal of Addiction. 1997;6:74-82.

7. First MB, Spitzer RL, Gibbon M, Williams JBW. Structured clinical interview for DSM-IV axis I disorders, clinician version (SCID-CV). Washington: American Psychiatric Press, Inc., 1997.

8. First MB, Spitzer RL, Gibbon M, Williams JBW. Structured clinical interview for DSM-IV axis I disorders, research version, patient edition with psychotic screen (SCID-I/P W/ PSY SCREEN). New York: Biometrics Research, New York State Psychiatric Institute, 1997.

9. Gastfriend DR, Lu SH, Sharon E. Placement matching: Challenges and technical progress. Subst Use Misuse. 2000;35:2191-213.

10. Turner WM, Turner KH, Reif S, et al. Feasibility of multidimensional substance abuse treatment matching: automating the ASAM patient placement criteria. Drug Alcohol Depend. 1999;55:35-43.

11. McLellan AT, Kushner H, Metzger D, et al. The fifth edition of the addiction severity index. J Subst Abuse Treat. 1992;9:199-213.

12. American Psychiatric Association. Diagnostic and statistical manual of mental disorders, fourth edition. Washington: American Psychiatric Association, 1994.

13. Finney JW, Moos RH, Humphreys K. A comparative evaluation of substance abuse treatment: II. Linking proximal outcomes of 12-step and cognitive-behavioral treatment to substance use outcomes. Alcohol Clin Exp Res. 1999;23:537-544.

14. Finney JW, Moos RH. Research report–entering treatment for alcohol abuse: A stress and coping model. Addiction. 1995;90:1223-1240.

15. Davis LJJ, Hoffmann NG, Morse RM, Luehr JG. Substance use disorder diagnostic schedule (SUDDS): The equivalence and validity of a computer-administered and an interviewer-administered format. Alcohol Clin Exp Res. 1992;16:250-254.

16. Buros Institute of Mental Measurements. Thirteenth mental measurements yearbook. Lincoln: University of Nebraska-Lincoln, 1999.

17. McLellan AT, Parikh G, Bragg A, et al. Addiction severity index (5th ed.). Philadelphia: Penn-VA Center for Studies of Addiction, 1990.

18. U.S. Government Department of Human Services. Form 90: A structured assessment interview for drinking and related behaviors, vol. 96-4004. WR Miller, ed. Washington: U.S. Government Department of Human Services, 1995.

19. Miller WR, Tonigan JS, Longabaugh R. The drinker inventory of consequences: an inventory for assessing adverse consequences of alcohol abuse. Test manual, vol. 4, project MATCH monograph series. Rockville: National Institute on Alcohol Abuse and Alcoholism, 1995.

20. Skinner HA, Horn HL. Alcohol dependence scale user's guide. Toronto: Addiction Research Foundation, 1984.

21. Skinner HA. Drug use questionnaire. Toronto: Addiction Research Foundation, 1982.

22. McGovern MP, Morrison DH. The chemical use, abuse and dependence scale (CUAD): Rationale, reliability and validity. J Subst Abuse Treat. 1992;9:27-38.

23. Rohsenow DJ. Drinking habits and expectancies about alcohol's effects for self versus others. J Consult Clin Psychol. 1983;51:752-756.

24. Rohsenow DJ. Alcohol effects questionnaire (1980). In: Allen JP, Columbus M, eds. Assessing alcohol problems: A guide for clinicians and researchers. National Institute on alcohol abuse and alcoholism, treatment handbook series 4, Bethesda: NIAAA, 1985.

25. Brown SA, Christiansen BA, Goldman MS. The alcohol expectancy questionnaire: An instrument for the assessment of adolescent and adult alcohol expectancies. J Stud Alcohol. 1987;48:483-491.

26. Brown SA. In: Allen JP, Columbus M, eds. Assessing alcohol problems: A guide for clinicians and researchers. National institute on alcohol abuse and alcoholism, treatment handbook series 4, Bethesda: NIAAA, 1995.

27. Anton RF, Moak DH, Latham PK. The obsessive compulsive drinking scale: A new method of assessing outcome in alcoholism treatment studies. Arch Gen Psych. 1996;53:225-231.

28. Roberts JS, Anton RF, Latham PK, Moak DH. Factor structure and predictive validity of the obsessive compulsive drinking scale. Alcohol Clin Exp Res. 1999; 23:1484-1491.

29. Annis HM, Graham JM, Davis CS. Inventory of drinking situations. Toronto: Addiction Research Foundation, 1987.

30. Turner NE, Annis HM, Sklar SM. Measurement of antecedents to drug and alcohol use: Psychometric properties of the inventory of drug-taking situations (IDTS). Behav Res Ther. 1997;35:465-483.

31. Annis HM, Graham JM. Situational confidence questionnaire. Toronto: Addiction Research Foundation, 1988.

32. Sarason IG, Johnson JH, Siegel JM. Assessing the impact of life changes: Development of the life experiences survey. J Consult Clin Psychol. 1978;46:932-946.

33. Donovan DM, O'Leary MR. The drinking-related locus of control scale. J Stud Alcohol. 1978;39:759-784.

34. Donovan DM, O'Leary MR. Control orientation, drinking behavior, and alcoholism. In: Lefcourt HM, ed. Research with the locus of control construct. New York: Academic Press, 1983;2:107-154.

35. Lefcourt HM. Locus of control. In: Robinson JP, Shaver PR, et al., eds. Measures of personality and social psychological attitudes. Measures of social psychological attitudes. San Diego: Academic Press, 1991;1:413-489.

36. Keyson J. Drinking-related locus of control scale. In: Allen JP, Columbus M, eds. Assessing alcohol problems: A guide for clinicians and researchers. National institute on alcohol abuse and alcoholism, treatment handbook series 4, Bethesda: NIAAA, 1995.

37. Bunch JM, Schneider HG. Smoking-specific locus of control. Psychol Rep. 1991;69:1075-1081.

38. Oswald LM, Walker GC, Reilly EL, et al. Measurement of locus of control in cocaine abusers. Issues in Mental Health Nursing. 1992;13:81-94.

39. Myers M, Brown S, Mott M. Coping as a predictor of substance abuse treatment outcome. J Subst Abuse. 1993;5:15-30.

40. DiClemente CC, Hughes SO. Stages of change profiles in outpatient alcoholism treatment. Journal of Substance Abuse. 1990;2:217-235.

41. Litman GK, Stapleton J, Oppenheim AN, Peleg M. An instrument for measuring coping behaviors in hospitalized alcoholics: Implications for relapse prevention and treatment. Br J Addict. 1983;78:269-276.

42. Litman GK, Stapleton J, Oppenheim AN, et al. The relationship between coping behaviors, their effectiveness and alcoholism relapse and survival. Br J Addict. 1984;79:283-291.

43. Lazarus RS, Folkman S. Stress, appraisal and coping. New York: Springer, 1984.

44. Folkman S, Lazarus RS, Dunkel-Schetter C, et al. Dynamics of a stressful encounter: Cognitive appraisal, coping, and encounter outcomes. J Pers Soc Psychol. 1986;50:992-1003.

45. Moos RH, Brennan PL, Fondacaro MR. Approach and avoidance coping responses among older problem and nonproblem drinkers. Psychol Aging. 1990;5:31-40.

46. Morey L. PAI: An overview of the personality assessment inventory. Odessa: Psychological Assessment Resources, 1992.

47. Cloninger CR, Svrakic DM, Przybeck TR. A psychobiological model of temperament and character. Arch Gen Psychiatry. 1993;50:975-990.

Development of Service Intensity Criteria and Program Categories for Individuals with Co-Occurring Disorders

Kenneth Minkoff, MD
Joan Zweben, PhD
Richard Rosenthal, MD
Richard Ries, MD

SUMMARY. Many patients present a clinical situation in which psychiatric symptomatology and substance related symptomatology are inextricably intertwined. A paradox exists for these patients, in that both the addictions and mental health systems of care, and the level of care assessment methodologies associated with each system, are designed for

Kenneth Minkoff is Medical Director, Arbour-Choate Health Management, Woburn, MA and is also affiliated with Harvard Medical School, Boston, MA.

Joan Zweben is Executive Director, East Bay Community Recovery Project & 14th Street Clinic, Berkeley, CA and is also affiliated with the University of California, San Francisco, CA.

Richard Rosenthal is Chairman, Department of Psychiatry, St. Luke's Roosevelt Hospital Center, New York, NY and is also affiliated with the Albert Einstein College of Medicine, NY.

Richard Ries is Director, Outpatient Mental Health Services Dual Disorder Programs, Harborview Medical Center, Seattle, WA and is also affiliated with the University of Washington Health Sciences.

Address correspondence to: Kenneth Minkoff, MD, 12 Jefferson Drive, Acton, MA 01720 (E-mail: Kminkov@aol.com).

[Haworth co-indexing entry note]: "Development of Service Intensity Criteria and Program Categories for Individuals with Co-Occurring Disorders." Minkoff, Kenneth et al. Co-published simultaneously in *Journal of Addictive Diseases* (The Haworth Medical Press, an imprint of The Haworth Press, Inc.) Vol. 22, Supplement No. 1, 2003, pp. 113-129; and: *Addiction Treatment Matching: Research Foundations of the American Society of Addiction Medicine (ASAM) Criteria* (ed: David R. Gastfriend) The Haworth Medical Press, an imprint of The Haworth Press, Inc., 2003, pp. 113-129. Single or multiple copies of this article are available for a fee from The Haworth Document Delivery Service [1-800-HAWORTH, 9:00 a.m. - 5:00 p.m. (EST). E-mail address: docdelivery@haworthpress.com].

http://www.haworthpress.com/store/product.asp?sku=J069
Digital Object Identifier: 10.1300/J069v22S01_08

one type of disorder only, or only one disorder at a time. As a result, these individuals are perceived as "system misfits." Our inability to assess these patients accurately and place them appropriately contributes to poor outcomes and high costs. These costs consist of expensive utilization of scarce system resources. There is a growing need for a more integrated methodology for level of care assessment, in which both psychiatric and substance symptomatology can be assessed simultaneously to generate a wider array of programmatic interventions for individuals with co-occurring disorders. This article describes efforts to build upon the Patient Placement Criteria published by the American Society of Addiction Medicine, Second Edition (ASAM PPC-2) to develop a revised instrument that is much more capable of evaluating the placement needs of individuals who present with combinations of psychiatric and substance symptomatology. *[Article copies available for a fee from The Haworth Document Delivery Service: 1-800-HAWORTH. E-mail address: <docdelivery@ haworthpress.com> Website: <http://www.HaworthPress.com> © 2003 by The Haworth Press, Inc. All rights reserved.]*

KEYWORDS. ASAM criteria, co-occurring disorders, comorbid disorders, dual diagnosis, treatment intensity

INTRODUCTION

A 57-year-old-divorced man with longstanding alcohol dependence is brought to the emergency room by his family. He has a blood alcohol level of .32, and complains of suicidal ideation. His family is eager for him to be admitted for alcohol treatment.

A 28-year-old prostitute who is HIV positive presents to a detoxification program seeking treatment for crack cocaine dependence. She reports to the intake worker that she "hears voices all the time."

A 34-year-old man with chronic disabling schizophrenia is brought by his case manager to a substance abuse treatment program for evaluation of his daily marijuana use and weekly episodes of alcohol intoxication. He reports to the evaluator that he knows he shouldn't use drugs, but he does not want to change. The case manager insists that he needs services.

Cases such as these are increasingly common in emergency service and acute care settings in both the mental health system and the addiction treatment system. Such cases present profound dilemmas for clinical evaluators attempting to perform a clinical crisis assessment to determine level of care and appropriate treatment program referral. The reason for this dilemma is quite simple: each of these cases presents a clinical situation in which psychiatric symptomatology and substance related symptomatology are inextricably intertwined. The paradox is that both our systems of care, and the level of care assessment methodologies used by each system, are designed as if individuals present primarily with one type of disorder only, or only one disorder at a time. As a result, these individuals are experienced as "system misfits." Our inability to assess them accurately and place them appropriately contributes to poor outcomes and high costs. These costs consist of expensive utilization of scarce system resources. Consequently, there is a growing need for a more integrated methodology for level of care assessment, in which both psychiatric and substance symptomatology can be assessed simultaneously. This article describes efforts to build upon the existing Patient Placement Criteria published by the American Society of Addiction Medicine, Second Edition (ASAM PPC-2)[1] to develop a revised instrument that is much more capable of evaluating the placement needs of individuals who present with combinations of psychiatric and substance symptomatology.

Plans for the revised instrument, the ASAM PPC-2R, began in 1997, with the formation of the Coalition for Clinical Criteria, under the leadership of David Mee-Lee, MD. The specific purpose of the Coalition was to develop a nationwide expert panel to assist with the development of patient placement criteria for individuals with co-occurring disorders. The initial development of the ASAM Patient Placement Criteria was intended to provide a scientifically rational basis for moving the addiction treatment field away from the notion that "one size fits all" (that is, all individuals with addiction should be referred to standard "28 Day" programs). The intention was to move toward individualized multidimensional assessment with assignment to one of four "levels of care." The development of PPC-2 in 1996 was intended to add complexity and sensitivity to the multidimensional level of care assessment process of the original ASAM Criteria, PPC-1.[2] This development included an expectation of increased capability to assess for comorbid psychiatric disorders and created a broader service array within each level of care. Despite these intentions, the application of PPC-2 in state level systems has continued to take place in addiction agencies focused on primary addiction, and there has been little, if any, formal acknowledgement of the presence of psychiatric illness and disability in either the assessment process or in program design. Consequently, the ASAM PPC-2 were unable to capture the range of clinical presentations (in both mental health and substance settings) suggested by the opening cases, and the program array described emphasized models that work with addiction only, and did not formally address significant psychiatric illness, symptomatology, or disability.

The development of ASAM PPC-2R, therefore, required the broader integration of mental health perspectives into what has hitherto been an "addiction only" instrument.[3] An important premise of our work on this project was to provide this broader perspective through incorporating available information about evidence based best practices[4] and clinical consensus principles and best practices[5,6] for the treatment of co-occurring disorders into existing models for level of care assessment and treatment program matching.

The first principle, based upon available epidemiologic data (see below), is that *dual diagnosis is an expectation, not an exception.* During the past two decades, there has been increasing recognition of the high prevalence of individuals with comorbid psychiatric and substance disorders presenting for services in both the mental health system and the addiction treatment system.[7,8] Consequently, although it was originally thought that the instrument we were creating would be a special "PPC-Dual," to supplement the existing PPC-2, it became clear that the prevalence of comorbidity would make the use of two documents extremely cumbersome. Consequently, the goal of the project became the *replacement* of PPC-2, with the expectation that the level of care assessment process needed to assume that co-occurring disorder was routinely present.

LITERATURE REVIEW

The initial assignment for the Coalition was to begin to incorporate already available research and pre-existing level of care assessment or utilization management tools into the ASAM PPC-2R development process.

Within the field of addiction treatment, the work of McLellan and others has demonstrated that when addiction is complicated by multiple problems in other dimensions (including comorbid psychiatric impairment), then multidimensional interventions produce better outcomes.[9-11] Moreover, it is the tightness of fit between the patient's problem profile and the services *actually* received that predicts improved outcome. This approach is called problem-service matching. This supports the approach of the PPC-2R workgroups to try to capture the multiple dimensions of complexity of the dually diagnosed patient, and specify the types of services that must be present to meet identified needs. If the patient can be placed in a setting that offers most of the needed services, s/he is much more likely to actually utilize them than if care is fragmented. Hence, treatment matching involves not only selection of a so-called "level" of care, but identification of specific components of treatment intensity required in each clinical dimension that comprise the specific types of programs available at that level.

Within the mental health system, demonstration projects investigating interventions for individuals with serious mental illness and substance disorder have identified evidence-based best practices that emphasize not specific programs or episodes of care but rather integrated intensive case management teams (e.g., Continuous Treatment Teams) which incorporate unconditional continuity, proactive outreach, and stage-specific treatment for individuals who are both disabled and pre-motivational.[4,12,13] There is also evidence supporting the value of modified addiction residential programs such as the modified Therapeutic Community (TC) in the treatment of individuals with co-occurring disorders,[14] as well as psychiatrically enhanced detoxification programs,[15] integrated outpatient programs,[16,17] and integrated acute inpatient settings.[18-20] Clinical consensus on best practices indicates that there is no single correct programmatic intervention for individuals with co-occurring disorders; rather, interventions must be matched according to the availability of continuing integrated treatment relationship, the specific diagnoses, phases of recovery, stages of change, level of baseline disability, available contingencies (e.g., legal), and assessment of level of care.[5,6,13] Consequently, the challenge of ASAM PPC-2R involved utilizing dimensional criteria to match to the full range of programmatic possibilities.

Within the field of utilization management, there was little available to guide the process. Preliminary criteria validity studies have supported the validity of PPC in making addiction placement determinations,[21] but no validity data are available regarding application to individuals with comorbid disorders. A national survey of managed care organizations (MCOs) in 1997 indicated significant absence of available utilization management criteria for co-occurring disorders.[22] The Level of Care Utilization System (LOCUS)[23] is a multidimensional psychiatric and addiction level of care assessment tool in which one dimension addresses comorbidity, but the instrument as a whole does not address the full range of variables that contribute to placement in substance abuse treatment for individuals with co-occurring disorders. The LOCUS does, however, suggest a mechanism for incorporating *psychiatric* dimensions of assessment (e.g., risk of harm, level of functioning) into the ASAM dimensional assessment. Another instrument, the Choate Outline for Intensity of Care Evaluation for Dual Disorders CHOICE-Dual,[19] served as a utilization management manual for a dual diagnosis case rate program, and describes reasonably specific behavioral markers for matching patients to various types of integrated programs, distinguished not by linear "levels of care," but rather by a multidimensional array of service intensities.

CONCEPTUAL FRAMEWORK

Build Upon PPC-2

Based upon the literature review, a conceptual framework for the PPC-2R began to emerge. First, it seemed clear that the general structure and format of the PPC-2 was applicable to psychiatric disorders as well as to substance disorders. Consequently, PPC-2R could be constructed using the basic conceptual framework of its predecessor, as follows.

Multidimensional Assessment: First, both addiction and psychiatric disorders require assessment of multiple dimensions to establish level of care. Specifically, the six dimensions of assessment of substance disorders were retained in PPC-2R: intoxication/withdrawal potential, biomedical complications, emotional/behavioral complications, readiness, relapse potential, and recovery environment. Then, within the emotional/behavioral dimension, specific dimensions of psychiatric assessment were enumerated.

An underlying principle that defined the dimensional approach was the concept of Multidimensional Risk, a probabilistic-actuarial point of view. Developing a multidimensional risk profile integrates all biopsychosocial data and history into a more succinct summary of symptom severity and functional impairment. (Although multidimensional risk is implicit in the construction of the PPC-2R , the approach of providing benchmarks for rating clinical risk and assigning thresholds for service intensity based upon risk intensity in each dimension is made explicit in the experimental assessment matrix included as an appendix to PPC-2R.)

Within the emotional/behavioral dimension, the following specific dimensions of psychiatric assessment were elaborated as Risk Domains and made explicit in PPC-2R:

1. *Dangerousness/Lethality.* This describes, in the context of impulsivity and capacity to act, the seriousness and immediacy of the individual's ideation, plans, and behavior with regard to homicide, suicide, or other forms of harm to self or others and/or to property.
2. *Interference with Addiction Recovery Efforts.* This describes the degree to which a patient is distracted from addiction recovery efforts by emotional, behavioral, and/or cognitive problems.
3. *Social Functioning.* This describes the degree to which an individual's relationships are affected by substance use and/or other emotional, behavioral, and cognitive problems.
4. *Ability for Self Care.* This describes the degree to which an individual's ability to perform activities of daily living are affected by his or her substance use and/or other emotional, behavioral, and cognitive problems.
5. *Course of Illness.* This encompasses history of the patient's illness and treatment response as a context to interpret current signs, symptoms and presentation and to support predicting the patient's treatment response.

Independent Categories of Service Intensity: Second, dimensions of assessment may *modify* service intensity for each disorder, once a disorder is conceptualized as being "de-linked" from level of care. This continues a process that began with PPC-2, in which multiple programs could be defined at each level of care, each with a varying array of service intensities matched to specific dimensional needs.

With regard to co-occurring disorders, therefore, appropriate treatment matching depends on evaluation of separate dimensions that predict particular service intensity requirements for *each* disorder. An example is an individual who meets addiction criteria for an addiction day treatment program, but who also has significant impairment of functioning due to a psychiatric disability. This patient will need either a specialized addiction day treatment program designed to accommodate individuals with psychiatric disabilities (see below) or, if such a program is unavailable, a higher level of care that combines needed psychiatric and substance-related treatment intensity.

Add Co-Occurring Disorder Specific Concepts

In addition to multidimensional assessment and de-linked independent categories of service intensity, the PPC-2R incorporates five constructs unique to co-occurring disorders: integrated dual primary treatment; subtyping of dual disorders based on acuity and disability, interactivity of level of care requirements; stage-specific treatment; and committability as a dimension of assessment.

Integrated Dual Primary Treatment: One of the key consensus best practice principles is that psychiatric and substance disorders are both primary when they co-occur, and each requires specific and appropriately intensive primary treatment in an integrated manner.[5,24] This principle alleviates the requirement to determine which disorder "came first," "caused the other," or "is most important." Within the structure of ASAM PPC-2R, the focus is on addressing two primary disorders simultaneously at any point in time, not worrying about presumed etiology. Consequently, the process of level of care assessment begins with identifying the most significant risk (medical or safety) connected with either condition, determining the matrix of service intensities required to address that risk, and then assessing the service intensity required to address the comorbid condition in that context.

Subtyping of Dual Disorders: During the past decade, it has become increasingly clear that individuals with co-occurring disorders vary tremendously in clinical presentation and clinical need.[25] Ries and Miller introduced a simple methodology for categorizing these individuals into four subtypes, based on high and low severity of mental illness and substance disorder.[26] This "four-box" model was incorporated into national consensus practice guidelines for co-occurring disorders, in which the "high severity" psychiatric disorders were identified as characteristic of individuals identified as seriously and persistently mentally ill (SPMI), and consequently eligible for priority services in the mental health system.[5] In the same year, a national conference of state mental health program directors and substance abuse directors[27] agreed to adopt a similar (though not identical) four-box model, the New York Model (adapted from References 28 and 29), as a national consensus for subtyping individuals with co-occurring disorders for state level service planning.[28,29]

Both models of subtyping indicate that service matching and programming go beyond mere presence of comorbidity and beyond specific diagnoses. Service matching depends on both acuity of symptomatology and severity of persistence and disability associated with either condition. These concepts were incorporated into the design of the PPC-2R. For any level of addiction treatment required, program matching must address low acuity, moderate acuity, and severe acuity (the latter usually requiring an acute psychiatric intervention), as well as low disability, moderate disability, and severe disability (the latter usually requiring integration of substance services into a psychiatric setting for individuals with severe and persistent mental illness) of the comorbid psychiatric disorder. The methodology for addressing this service matching paradigm within addiction programming is discussed further below, in the section on Program Categories.

Interactivity of Level of Care Requirements: The PPC-2 routinely incorporated emotional/behavioral complications *of addiction* into determination of service intensity requirements for *addiction* treatment. PPC-2R goes much further. In this document, level of care requirements for the treatment of each of two primary disorders can be identified, and then the resultant level of care for the combined condition can be derived from the presumed interactivity between the two disorders. As a consequence, the required level of care for the combined condition can be *higher* than what would be required for each condition considered separately.

Another issue of interactivity that is addressed in PPC-2R is the interaction between low motivation and other dimensions of assessment in the determination of level of care. This issue is best illustrated in the discussion of stage-specific treatment.

Stage-Specific Treatment: In the traditional unidimensional approach to treatment matching for addiction, individuals being assessed for addiction treatment services arrive because they have accepted (with more or less external coercion) that they need to enter addiction treatment in some fashion. In this context, low motivation is associated with a need for more intensively structured treatment interventions to promote treatment adherence and overcome denial. In the years since the release of PPC-2, however, the emergence of motivational enhancement technology in the addiction field[30] has made it clear that interventions need to be matched to stage of change (pre-contemplation, contemplation, preparation, action, maintenance).[31] For many "pre-contemplative" individuals who come to the attention of addiction clinicians, therefore, *less* intensive, rather than more intensive, interventions are needed to promote opportunities to enhance motivation through confrontation with negative consequences during the individual's efforts at harm reduction through reduced use or controlled use.

The literature on the value of stage-specific treatment and motivational enhancement is especially compelling in assessing level of care requirements for individuals with co-occurring disorders, particularly those with severe mental illness.

Early researchers on integrated services for individuals with SPMI and substance disorders identified four stages of treatment: engagement, persuasion (motivational enhancement), active treatment, and relapse prevention.[32] Investigation of intensive integrated ambulatory case management team treatment approaches has demonstrated the value of "stagewise" treatment in promoting progress,[33] particularly given that these individuals become attached to treatment due to their *mental illnesses*, even though they may have no interest whatsoever in addressing substance use as a problem. Carey[34] and Ziedonis and Trudeau[35] have demonstrated that application of motivational enhancement strategies can be as effective with individuals with chronic psychoses at baseline as for individuals with no mental illness. Consequently, treatment matching paradigms in PPC-2R now suggest that individuals with psychiatric disabilities who have low motivation for substance disorder treatment be "placed" in integrated outpatient case management programs with stage-specific motivational enhancement interventions, rather than routinely referred to expensive residential treatment environments, as would result from application of PPC-2. The major exception to this rule relates to the application of mental health committability criteria, which will be discussed in the next section.

Committability: Committability is defined as meeting the legal standard (as defined by states) for involuntary psychiatric treatment. Incorporation of psychiatric committability as a variable in PPC-2R represents a significant step in the direction of a fully integrated level of care assessment tool. The key distinction occurs in dimension 4, where individuals who are most highly treatment resistant are divided into two groups, one in which continued active use, while risky, is not associated with the imminent danger that warrants committability, and one in which committability criteria are met. In the former situation, outpatient based motivational enhancement interventions are indicated; in the latter situation, involuntary psychiatric hospitalization (ideally on a dual diagnosis unit) is required. This illustrates that placement decisions do not always reflect a linear relationship between particular dimensions of assessment and degrees of service intensity. Rather, there are occasions in which a change in a single variable results in placement in a radically different setting and/or level of care.

This conceptual framework clearly permits more sensitivity to the complexity of co-occurring disorders in the level of care assessment and placement process. However, it soon became apparent that identification of specialized service needs would not be terribly helpful unless there was a corresponding increase in the complexity of the service array to which patients could be referred. This realization led to the development of the concept of "program categories," which is discussed in the next section.

PROGRAM CATEGORIES

As the PPC-2R evolved, it became increasingly clear that the higher levels of severity of psychiatric acuity and disability described in dimension 3 could not be routinely accommodated in a typical addiction program, regardless of level of care. At the same time, the workgroup recognized that many addiction programs continue to have essentially no capacity to accommodate even mild impairments related to psychiatric illness. As a consequence, addiction programming in the service array at each level of care was divided into three categories: *Dual Diagnosis Capable (DDC); Dual Diagnosis Enhanced (DDE); and Addiction Only Services (AOS).*

DDC: Although previous versions of the ASAM Criteria have discussed the importance of assessing and addressing emotional/behavioral issues in the context of routine addiction treatment interventions, the criteria to date have *not* implied a requirement that addiction programs routinely demonstrate formal capability in assessment and treatment of co-occurring psychiatric disorders. In PPC-2R, however, this has changed dramatically, and this change represents a major innovation for the entire addiction treatment field. PPC-2R asserts the following: *All standard addiction programs, at all levels of care, are expected to demonstrate formally measurable dual diagnosis capability (DDC) status.* For the first time, there are documented basic standards to govern the manner in which addiction programs must deal with psychiatric comorbidity.

The specifics of Dual Diagnosis Capability are as follows: DDC programming at each level of care routinely welcomes and appropriately treats individuals with co-occurring disorders, provided that those disorders are associated with acuity and disability that are sufficiently limited that they can be accommodated readily within the usual staffing, funding, and expectations of that addiction program at that level of care.

For a program to be designated as DDC it needs to meet measurable criteria by which DDC status can be documented, whether by site audit, chart review, or other quality monitoring procedures. DDC programs will have formal mission statements or treatment philosophies that document a welcoming message to individuals with co-occurring disorders. There will be routine methods for screening all admissions for mental illness symptoms, and providing a formal diagnostic mental health assessment for those who are "positive" on screening. When a mental illness diagnosis is identified, it is documented as an additional primary diagnosis, and identified as a primary problem, with specific goals and interventions, on the treatment plan. DDC programs have policies and procedures to both ensure, and explicitly encourage, medication compliance, and have regularly scheduled groups to educate all clients about mental illness, its treatment, and the acceptance of prescribed medication for mental illness within the recovery community. In addition, staff have identified basic competencies in addressing mental illness issues listed above, as well as having access to an on-site supervisor with mental health training or licensure, and access to psychiatric or senior mental health consultation, the input of which is integrated into treatment record documentation.

DDE: Dual diagnosis enhanced programs are addiction programs, at any level of care, that have the ability to provide addiction treatment to individuals with comorbid psychiatric disorders who have *moderate acuity* (e.g., an individual in early recovery who experiences periodic impulses to harm herself when under stress and experiencing flashbacks of early traumatic memories) or *moderate disability* (e.g., an individual with chronic schizophrenia, motivated for addiction treatment, but whose participation in groups is impaired by virtue of persistent auditory hallucinations). These programs are one example of "integrated treatment programs," in which addiction and psychiatric treatment are combined in a single treatment setting and treatment team.

Previously, addiction programs with significant integration of mental health capability have not been identified specifically in the matrix of services delineated by the Patient Placement Criteria. However, in PPC-2R, there is, once again, a significant departure from the past. PPC-2R states: *In any system of care, at each level of care, the system should ensure adequate capacity of dual diagnosis enhanced treatment services.* These DDE services could be provided in a freestanding setting, or identified as a *component* of an existing DDC program. Examples of DDE programs include specialized outpatient,[16] IOP/partial hospitalization,[19] or residential programs (e.g., modified therapeutic community),[14] that provide substance disorder treatment services geared toward individuals with moderately severe psychiatric impairment.

For a program to meet DDE criteria, it must first meet all DDC criteria, and, in addition, have staff with higher levels of mental illness competency, with more onsite supervision, and formal inclusion of psychiatric time (usually, on site) in assessment, treatment planning, and treatment interventions. DDE programs are more expensive than DDC programs because they incorporate higher levels of staffing, often with more advanced degrees, involve smaller groups, at a slower pace, with more modification of educational interventions to address the learning limitations of individuals with significant disability or distraction.[36] DDE programs also have groups with more mental health content integrated into the group program, formal procedures for communication, referral, care coordination, and continuity of care with mental health providers, and more capacity to maintain treatment continuity (even if in another setting or level of care) if the patient slips or lapses.

AOS: Addiction-only services, formerly the mainstay of addiction treatment systems, are validated, but dramatically de-emphasized, in PPC-2R. PPC-2R states: Addiction-only services continue to exist in most systems, but over time they will be less and less relevant, and will be serving a dwindling share of the total cohort of addiction patients in most communities. To underscore this point, AOS services are deliberately omitted from the service matrix in PPC-2R. At each level of care, matched services are designated DDC or DDE, depending on the psychiatric needs of the population served.

CONCLUSION

ASAM PPC-2R has built upon accumulating data that supports evidence based best practices in the addiction field, the mental health field, and the utilization management field. This effort has sought to develop a paradigm for multidimensional service intensity assessment for individuals presenting with substance-related problems who also have a wide range of comorbid psychiatric symptoms, disorders, and impairments. This paradigm is supported by a new conceptualization of program categories within a comprehensive array of addiction services in a system of care: Dual Diagnosis Capable, Dual Diagnosis Enhanced, and Addiction Only Services. These categories encourage programs and systems to design interventions that more effectively match the multidimensional needs of individuals with co-occurring disorders.

Although this model is built upon, and derives from, evidence based best practice, there is little, if any, data that support the model itself. A key area for future research, utilizing the PPC-2R, will be to investigate the reliability and validity of the assessment criteria and the program categories for the purpose of improving accuracy of treatment matching, the effectiveness of program design, the efficiency of system development, and ultimately, the quality of clinical outcomes for individuals with co-occurring disorders.

Nonetheless, the PPC-2R is likely to have a profound impact on the overall capacity of the addiction treatment system to address the needs of individuals with co-occurring disorders. For the first time, there is a nationally recognized set of standards defining minimal, measurable program competencies for addiction programs with regard to comorbid psychiatric conditions. Minkoff has begun to apply the DDC and DDE program categories beyond the chemical dependence (CD) system to the mental health (MH) system as well, extending the work of the managed care initiative consensus panel of the Substance Abuse Mental Health Services Administration[5] to assert that all mental health programs should demonstrate basic dual diagnosis capability, using similar measurable criteria to those used for addiction programs.[6] In addition, Minkoff recommends that mental health systems attempt to develop DDE mental health program capacity for each type of program (e.g., inpatient psychiatry, day treatment, mental health residential) in the system of care. Thus, the array of program categories in a comprehensive, continuous, integrated system of care will include DDC-CD, DDE-CD, DDC-MH, and DDE-MH programs. As these standards become more widely available, it is likely that they might be incorporated into state regulations and licensure requirements, as well as payor program standards for reimbursement purposes. Further, for the first time, the addiction system can identify standards for defining a model of addiction treatment (DDE standards) specifically intended to provide integrated services in addiction settings to individuals with unstable or disabling comorbid conditions. This is likely to facilitate both the development and funding of new DDE program models at all levels of care. Finally, the availability of "integrated" level of care assessment materials and utilization management standards may affect utilization management practices in both public and private managed care systems. Many MCOs currently use ASAM Criteria as the basis for their addiction-specific utilization management procedures. If these same MCOs begin to develop utilization management procedures based on PPC-2R, this will lead to significant progress in creating care management practices that are more sensitive to the interactive needs of individuals with co-occurring disorders.

REFERENCES

1. American Society of Addiction Medicine. Patient placement criteria for the treatment of substance-related disorders. Chevy Chase, American Society of Addiction Medicine, Inc., 1996.

2. Hoffmann N, Halikas J, Mee-Lee D, Weedman R. American Society of Addiction Medicine Patient Placement Criteria for the treatment of psychoactive substance use disorders. Washington, American Society of Addiction Medicine, Inc., 1991.

3. Mee-Lee D, Shulman GD, Fishman M, et al. eds. ASAM Patient Placement Criteria for the Treatment of Substance-Related Disorders, Second Edition-Revised (ASAM PPC-2R). Chevy Chase, American Society of Addiction Medicine, Inc., 2001.

4. Drake RE, Essock S, Shaner A, et al. Implementing dual diagnosis services for clients with severe mental illness. Psych Serv. 2001;52:469-476.

5. Minkoff K. Center for Mental Health Services Managed Care Initiative Panel on Co-Occurring Disorders: Individuals with co-occurring psychiatric and substance disorders in managed care systems: standards of care, practice guidelines, workforce competencies, and training curricula. Rockville, Center for Mental Health Services, 1998.

6. Minkoff K. An integrated model for the management of co-occurring psychiatric and substance disorders in managed-care systems. Dis Mgt & H Outc. 2000;8: 251-257.

7. Regier DA, Farmer ME, Rae DS, et al. Comorbidity of mental disorders with alcohol and other drug abuse. JAMA. 1990;264:2511-2518.

8. Kessler RC, Nelson CB, McGonagle KA, et al. The epidemiology of co-occurring mental and addictive disorders: Implications for prevention and service utilization. Am J Orthopsy. 1996;66:17-31.

9. McLellan AT, Grissom GR, Brill P, et al. Private substance abuse treatments: Are some programs more effective than others? J Sub Ab Tr. 1993;10:243-254.

10. McLellan AT, Grissom GR, Zanis D, et al. Problem-service matching in addiction treatment. Arch Gen Psych. 1997;54:730-735.

11. McLellan AT, Hagan TA, Levine M, et al. Supplemental social services improve outcomes in public addiction treatment. Addiction. 1998;93:1489-1499.

12. Ries RK, Comtois K, Roy-Byrne PP. Illness severity and treatment services for dually diagnosed severely mentally ill outpatients. Schiz Bull. 1997;23:239-246.

13. Wingerson D, Ries RK. Assertive community treatment for patients with chronic and severe mental illness who abuse drugs. J Psych Drugs. 1999;31:13-18.

14. Sacks S, Sacks JY, De Leon G. Treatment for MICAs: Design and implementation of the modified TC. J Psych Drugs. 1999;31:19-30.

15. Wilens T, O'Keefe J, O'Connell JJ. A public dual diagnosis detoxification unit–Part 1: Organization and structure. Am J Add. 1993;2:91-98.

16. Rosenthal RN, Hellerstein DJ, Miner CR. A model of integrated services for outpatient treatment of patients with comorbid schizophrenia and addictive disorders. Am J Add. 1992;1:339-348.

17. Rosenthal RN. Hellerstein DJ, Miner CR. Integrated services for treatment of schizophrenic substance abusers: Demographics, symptoms, and substance abuse patterns. Psych Quart. 1992;63:3-26.

18. Minkoff, K. An integrated treatment model for dual diagnosis of psychosis and addiction. Hosp Comm Psych. 1989;40:1031-1036.

19. Minkoff K, Regner J. Innovations in integrated dual diagnosis treatment in public managed care: The Choate dual diagnosis case rate program. J Psych Drugs. 1999;31:3-11.

20. Ries RK, Russo J, Wingerson D, et al. Shorter hospital stays and more rapid improvement among patients with schizophrenia and substance disorders. Psych Serv. 2000;51:210-215.

21. Turner WM, Turner KH, Reif S, et al. Feasibility of multidimensional substance abuse treatment matching: Automating the ASAM Patient Placement Criteria. Drug Alc Dep. 1999;55:35-43.

22. Minkoff K. Center for Mental Health Services Managed Care Initiative Panel on Co-Occurring Disorders. Annotated bibliography. Rockville, Center for Mental Health Services, 1997.

23. American Association of Community Psychiatrists (AACP). Level of care utilization system (LOCUS). Dallas, American Association of Community Psychiatrists, 1998.

24. Ries RK, ed. Assessment and treatment of patients with co-existing mental illness and alcohol and other drug abuse. Treatment Improvement Protocol (TIP) Series, Number 9. Rockville, Center for Substance Abuse Treatment, 1994.

25. Lehman AF, Myers CP, Dixon LB, Johnson JL. Defining subgroups of dual diagnosis patients for service planning. Hosp Comm Psych. 1994;45:556-561.

26. Ries RK, Miller, NS. Dual diagnosis: Concept, diagnosis, and treatment. In: Dunner DL, ed. Current psychiatric therapy. Philadelphia, WB Saunders, 1993:131-138.

27. National Association of State Mental Health Program Directors, National Association of State Alcohol and Drug Abuse Directors. National dialogue on co-occurring mental health and substance abuse disorders. Washington, DC. June 15-17, 1998.

28. Rosenthal RN. Mental illness/chemical addiction: A guide to emergency services assessment and treatment. Albany, NY State Office of Mental Health, Division of Clinical Support Systems, 1993.

29. Rosenthal RN, Westreich L. Treatment of persons with dual diagnoses of substance use disorder and other psychological problems. In: McCrady BS, Epstein EE, eds. Addictions: A comprehensive guidebook. New York, Oxford University Press, 1999.

30. Miller WR, Rollnick, S. Motivational Interviewing. New York, Guilford, 1991.

31. Prochaska JO, DiClemente CC, Norcross JC. In search of how people change: Applications to addictive behavior. Am Psychol. 1992;47:1102-1114.

32. Osher FC, Kofoed L. Treatment of patients with psychiatric and substance use disorders. Hosp Comm Psych. 1989;40:1025-1030.

33. Drake RE, Bartels SB, Teague GB, et al. Treatment of substance use disorders in severely mentally ill patients. J Nerv Ment Dis. 1993;181:606-611.

34. Carey K. Treatment of co-occurring substance abuse and major mental illness. In: Drake RE & Mueser KT, eds. Dual diagnosis of major mental illness and substance

abuse. Volume II: Recent research and clinical implications. San Francisco, Jossey-Bass, 1996.

35. Ziedonis DM, Trudeau K. Motivation to quit using substances among individuals with schizophrenia: Implications for a motivation-based treatment model. Schiz Bull. 1997;23:229-238.

36. Roberts LJ, Shaner A, Eckman TA. Overcoming addictions: Skills training for people with schizophrenia. New York, WW Norton, 1999.

Feasibility of Multidimensional Substance Abuse Treatment Matching: Automating the ASAM Patient Placement Criteria

Winston M. Turner, PhD
Kingsley H. Turner
Sharon Reif
William E. Gutowski, PhD
David R. Gastfriend, MD

Winston M. Turner, Kingsley H. Turner, Sharon Reif, and David R. Gastfriend are affiliated with the Addiction Research Program, Department of Psychiatry, Massachusetts General Hospital and Harvard Medical School.

William E. Gutowski is affiliated with the Delta/Sigma Measurement and Decision Group.

Address correspondence to: David R. Gastfriend, MD, Director, Addiction Research Program, Massachusetts General Hospital, 16 Parkman Street, Boston, MA 02114 (E-mail: dgastfriend@partners.org).

The authors would like to thank the members of the Expert Review Panel for their important contribution to the criteria mapping process: Joseph Frawley, MD (CA Society of Addiction Medicine and ASAM); Norman Hoffmann, PhD (ASAM Criteria co-author); David Mee-Lee, MD (ASAM Criteria co-author); Michael Miller, MD (Joint Commission on Accreditation of Healthcare Organizations, American Medical Association and ASAM Committees); Kenneth Minkoff, MD (American Academy of Addiction Psychiatrists and expert clinician); and Alan Wartenberg, MD (ASAM Criteria Validity Study participant and expert clinician). In addition, the authors wish to acknowledge the collaborating sponsors of this study: (1) Massachusetts Department of Public Health/Bureau of Substance Abuse Services, Mayra Rodriguez-Howard, MSW, Director, and (2) Massachusetts Behavioral Health Partnership, Inc., Meg Anzalone, PhD, Vice President of Quality Management. Special thanks to Research Assistants Donna Janas, MA, Jonn Riordan and Jennifer Vickers, MA, of Massachusetts General Hospital.

This research was made possible through grants from the National Institute on Drug Abuse (NIDA Grant # DA08781) and the Massachusetts Bureau of Substance Abuse.

Reprinted with permission from *Drug & Alcohol Dependence*, 55:35-43, Turner, Turner, Reif, Gutowski, and Gastfriend, "Feasibility of Multidimensional Substance Abuse Treatment Matching: Automating the ASAM Patient Placement Criteria," copyright 1999, Elsevier Ireland Ltd.

SUMMARY. The Patient Placement Criteria published by the American Society of Addiction Medicine (ASAM Criteria) established a nonproprietary standard for matching substance use disorder patients to treatment settings.

Methods: Data from 593 substance dependent adults who were assessed using the first computerized implementation of the ASAM Criteria were analyzed to determine whether level of care assignments showed significant differences on a variety of clinical measures.

Results: The algorithm showed acceptable discrimination between each of three ASAM Levels of Care across numerous clinical subscales.

Conclusions: It is feasible to implement complex, multidimensional criteria for substance abuse treatment that may improve reliability and facilitate validity studies. *[Article copies available for a fee from The Haworth Document Delivery Service: 1-800-HAWORTH. E-mail address: <docdelivery@ haworthpress.com> Website: <http://www.HaworthPress.com>]*

KEYWORDS. Addiction, algorithm, automation, criteria, matching, substance abuse

INTRODUCTION

History of Patient Placement Criteria

During the 1980s, both the onset of cost pressures and the evolution of managed care resulted in the creation of 40 to 50 individual sets of addictions treatment matching protocols that were often developed as exclusive efforts by managed care entities (Center for Substance Abuse Treatment 1995). As a result, most were not released for public use and were utilized without testing their predictive validity. In a public effort to produce a set of placement criteria, the National Association of Addiction Treatment Providers (NAATP) and American Society of Addiction Medicine (ASAM) combined efforts to develop the first edition of the ASAM Patient Placement Criteria, published in 1991 (Hoffmann et al. 1991). The ASAM Criteria allow the clinician to systematically evaluate the severity of a patient's need for treatment along the six dimensions outlined in Table 1, and then utilizes a fixed combination rule to determine which of four levels of care a substance abusing patient will respond to with the greatest success. These levels are defined in Table 2.

TABLE 1. Assessment Dimensions

	Dimension	Dimension assesses:
Dimension 1	Acute Intoxication and/or Withdrawal Potential	Significant risk of severe withdrawal symptoms or seizures based on patient's previous withdrawal history, amount, frequency and recency of discontinuation or significant reduction of alcohol or other drug use
Dimension 2	Biomedical Conditions and Complications	Any acute or chronic medical issues that might possibly interfere with the current treatment episode
Dimension 3	Emotional/Behavioral Conditions and Complications	Any current psychiatric issues, including any behavioral or emotional problems that may impede the treatment process.
Dimension 4	Treatment Acceptance/Resistance	Patient's openness to treatment, acceptance of addiction, readiness for change, motivation for compliance and feelings of coercion.
Dimension 5	Relapse Potential	Patient's ability to cope with cravings, comprehension of relapse triggers and ability to abstain.
Dimension 6	Recovery Environment	Current living situation, adequacy of social support network, financial resources, etc.

TABLE 2. Dimensional Specifications for Admission to Level of Care

Level IV, *Medically managed intensive inpatient treatment*	At least one of Dimensions 1, 2 or 3 meet Level IV.
Level III, *Medically monitored intensive inpatient treatment*	At least two of the 6 Dimensions meet Level III criteria.
Level II, *Intensive outpatient treatment*	One of Dimensions 3-6 meet Level II *and* Dimensions 1 and 2 are no higher than Level II.
Level I, *Outpatient treatment*	All 6 Dimensions meet Level I criteria.

Reliability and Validity Challenges

To date, the validity of the ASAM PPC has not been prospectively demonstrated (Morey 1996), leaving the ASAM Criteria open to criticism by managed care (Book et al. 1995). The only validation attempt published to date is a retrospective test of a partial implementation. In that study, McKay et al. demonstrated modest predictive validity on the psychosocial dimensions but did not test the biomedical or withdrawal dimensions (McKay et al. 1997).

The validity of any assessment system is, ultimately, strongly dependent upon the reliable use of that system by clinicians functioning under typical clinical circumstances. The complexity of the ASAM Criteria raises serious questions about whether acceptable levels of reliability are attainable by the average clinician. The large body of research literature on human judgment and decision making (Pitz et al. 1984; Hogarth 1987) clearly establishes that human decision processes seldom, if ever, follow the prescriptions of explicit or formal models such as placement criteria, even in simple situations. Rather, these studies indicate that treatment choices inevitably will involve constructive processing (Payne et al. 1992) in which clinicians use flexible strategies to integrate constantly changing beliefs and knowledge.

Complex chronic disease states such as addictions offer nearly overwhelming amounts of data that must be adaptively managed (Miller 1956). Judgment strategies are necessary to resolve the inevitable accuracy/effort tradeoff that clinical decision makers face (Bartlett 1932). human preferences and, similarly, clinical decisions are seldom, if ever, generated by objective, consistent algorithms (Tversky et al. 1988), and instead typically involve the use of strategies that are shaped, or biased, by experience (de Groot 1965). Moreover, there is considerable research demonstrating that experience does not necessarily improve clinical decision making (Garb 1989) and usually is inferior to actuarially based decisions (Dawes et al. 1974). An example of this is the slow adoption of naltrexone in alcoholism pharmacotherapy despite research data documenting its safety and efficacy (O'Malley et al. 1992; Volpicelli et al. 1992). In fact, even experts appear to have difficulty with optimal use of information in the case of unusual patterns of data (Goldberg 1969). These findings on the limitations of clinical decision making are often not well received by mental health clinicians (Holt 1986). However, the failure to learn from experience is quite a general phenomenon (Brehmer 1986), naturally arising from the fact that the feedback available to clinicians in non-research settings is structured in such a way that objective learning is extremely difficult, if not impossible to achieve (Hogarth 1987). Overall, these findings suggest that it is implausible for even experienced clinicians to consistently apply the complex rules involved in an intricate algorithm. Clearly, this complicates the process of evaluating the validity of protocols such as the ASAM Criteria. For these reasons, the use of decision aids or algorithms can aid and improve human judgement (von Winterfeldt et al. 1986). Many clinical studies have shown that expert system decision aids improve decisions (Schwartz et al. 1986) by eliminating context effects, emotional- and effort-related factors, or by simplifying information integration (Dawes et al., 1989; Kleinmuntz 1990).

These considerations should give pause to the field of addictions treatment during an era of intense scrutiny. The absence of valid criteria and the cognitive performance obstacles to reliable implementation of criteria pose a challenge to providers and payors alike. These concerns motivated the development of a computerized decision making algorithm that automatically performs the complex information integration required by the ASAM Criteria. The further purpose of this algorithm development was to facilitate a controlled, randomized clinical trial, the NIDA-funded ASAM Criteria Validity Study (Gastfriend & McLellan 1997).

METHODS

Decision Analysis: In order to automate the ASAM Criteria, a decision analysis was performed to determine the number of overt component decisions, i.e., as published in the 1991 ASAM Criteria. Next, any complex or compound decision rules were logically divided into their components. Compound rules might require summary decisions, e.g., "are conditions A, B and C present?" or exclusive decisions, e.g., "is condition A present but not condition B?" Once decision rules were divided into their elemental components, these components were then converted into simple items that could yield an affirmative or negative answer for each decision point, in essence reducing each item to a binary logic problem. This was accomplished by primarily borrowing question items from existing data collection instruments that could serve as feeders to the automated process. Since this was a research project which was testing the validity of the criteria, question items from several standard assessment instruments with known parametric properties were mapped to fit the ASAM criteria. All of the original instruments were included in their entirety so as to retain their psychometric integrity, although not all of their items were utilized in the mapping process. The Global Assessment of Function was also included in the computerized version of the assessment package as part of the research protocol along with a battery of paper-and-pencil, self-report questionnaires, but data from those measures were not utilized in the algorithm.

A multidisciplinary group of clinicians and researchers at the Addiction Services of Massachusetts General Hospital met for three hours per week over twelve weeks to choose items and assign weights for all decision points in the map. The instruments that were chosen as feeders for the criteria are listed in Figure 1.

FIGURE 1. Standardized Assessment Instruments Used to Implement the ASAM Criteria and Their Proportional Contribution to Decision Points in the Algorithm

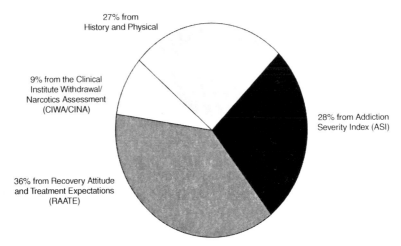

Some decision points, which primarily evaluated medical history, required the creation of supplemental medical status items. Many of the items mapped to the PPC were continuous measures which required that acceptable ranges be delineated to reduce these items to a binary decision format. Frequently, several items were selected from different instruments to address a specific criterion within the PPC, in which case a final judgment was algebraically derived from the individual items.

Review of Algorithm Mapping: Once the mapping process was completed, the results were distributed for review to a panel of expert clinicians who had experience with the ASAM Criteria and were participants in relevant professional organizations (see acknowledgements). The panelists were consulted for further refinement and adjustments to the map in an iterative process to assure that the map conformed to the format and content of the ASAM Criteria decision rules, *as published.*

Computer Implementation: Once approved through iterative revisions, the mapped decision points and scoring algorithm were programmed using the dBASE programming language and database management system. Feeder instruments were formatted onto computer displays for easy data entry by a research assistant or clinician conducting an assessment interview. All of the requisite questions are displayed, along with the appropriate codes for scoring each item. The result was an easy to use computerized patient assessment system that automated the ASAM Criteria using a laptop PC type computer running the DOS operating system.

After a training phase, the automated algorithm was evaluated for the mean duration of administration in patient care settings across multiple subjects by multiple interviewers. Laptop computers were programmed to record start and finish times for the process of administering questions and entering responses to all interview items. The algorithm was also subjected to inter-rater reliability testing, the methods and analysis of which will be reported elsewhere (Baker et al., 2003).

As a preliminary step toward establishing the concurrent validity of the ASAM Criteria, the algorithm was administered to a large, multi-site sample of addiction patients to obtain the ASAM Criteria assignments to intensive Levels of Care II, III and IV (subjects were not recruited from Level I outpatient settings or eligible for Level I due to the design and subject exclusion criteria of the ASAM Criteria Validity Study). These Level of Care groupings were then compared to subscale scores from the feeder instruments to determine if the algorithm generates distinct profiles for the patients who qualify for each level of treatment or whether no consistent pattern of subscale differences occurs. This is but a preliminary test, since ideally, concurrent validity requires comparison with independent measures that purport to assess the same construct. While it may seem tautological to utilize data from the input instruments to make the assessment in the first place and then examine those instruments to determine if the algorithm distinguishes the different Levels of Care, it is important to realize that only *individual items* from those instruments were mapped to the ASAM Criteria, not composite scores or subscale scores. Therefore, since these composite and subscale scores are conveniently gathered through the interview process, an initial comparison to these was made to evaluate the algorithm. Once group means within the Levels of Care were obtained, their differences were analyzed within each subscale using one-way analysis of variance with post-hoc Scheffe's test.

RESULTS

Decision Analysis of the ASAM Criteria and Implementation

When each dimension of the published ASAM Criteria was analyzed for overt decision points, the number of overt decisions for each dimension was as follows: Dimension 1 (Intoxication/Withdrawal): 46; Dimension 2 (Biomedical Conditions and Complications): 18; Dimension 3 (Emotional/Behavioral Conditions and Complications): 24; Dimension 4 (Treatment Acceptance/Resistance): 7; Dimension 5 (Relapse Potential): 10; Dimension 6 (Recovery Environment): 16. In sum, the raw decision rules were found to require 121 individual assessments across the six dimensions to derive a solution from among the four levels of care.

Within the 121 overt decision points, however, there were found to be numerous compound rules. These occur in criteria that contain compound phrases such as "and," "or," "but," "unless," etc., and which require that each sub-criterion be assessed as well. Reduction of compound decision rules resulted in a new matrix of 266 elemental decision points that require assessment before the final placement algorithm could be solved.

Question items selected from research instruments were found to satisfy the assessment requirements for approximately 73% of the 266 elemental decision items in the ASAM Criteria (see Figure 1). The remaining decision elements required the creation of some new question items to gather the specific history and current medical status data required for the algorithm. The item map that resulted from the complete process is contained in a 40-page spreadsheet.

Clinical Evaluation of the ASAM Criteria Computerized Algorithm

Data were gathered from all subjects enrolled in the ASAM Criteria Validity Study to date (N = 343) and additional volunteer "naturalistic" subjects who were willing to sit for the assessment interview but were ineligible for the randomized study (N = 250), for a combined data set of 593. All subjects were adults, self-identified as alcohol or drug dependent, treatment-seeking, English speaking and able to provide informed consent. Sixty-seven percent (N = 399) of the sample was male with a mean age of 36.6 years (range = 18-72). The majority of the subjects were Caucasian (66%), with 26% African American, 7% Latino and 1% from other racial/ethnic groups. Nearly half (44%) were either currently married or had been married in the past, and the remainder (56%) had never been married. The mean educational achievement was 12.2 years, with 72% of the subjects reporting having completed high school. Only 38% of the sample reported having any insurance coverage and 24% reported Medicaid coverage.

Substance preferences indicated a diverse sample. Many (42%) described regularly using both alcohol and drugs, but 21% were primarily alcoholics, 14% were primary heroin users, and 9% were primary cocaine users. However, in the previous month 57.5% reported drinking alcohol to intoxication, 28.5% reported using heroin and 50.6% reported using cocaine at least once.

Dimensional Specifications and Logic Gaps: Table 2 shows the Dimensional Specifications for Admission outlined in the Criteria. Review of these specifications reveals that certain logic gaps exist such that 20% of subjects failed to meet any of the criteria and assignment could not be reached, in essence allowing some subjects to "slip through the cracks." For example, for subjects whose rating for Dimension 1 or 2 is equal to Level III but none of Dimensions 3-6 equal Level III, the criteria for assignment to Level II care is violated. However, as only one of Dimensions 1-6 is equal to III, not two as specified by the Level III criteria, the subject does not qualify for Level III care either. This condition necessitated the creation of a default rule which assigned these unresolved cases to Level II care. Such defaults were approved and authorized by the external review panel as representing the intent of the ASAM criteria as published. Using such default conditions, the final distribution of subjects among the three eligible ASAM Levels of Care was as follows: 162 subjects (27.3%) were assigned to Level II, 337 subjects (56.8%) were assigned to Level III, and 94 subjects (15.9%) were assigned to Level IV.

Feasibility: Duration of administration by trained interviewers using laptop computers was assessed in the 593 subjects. The administration time for the entire research enrollment protocol required approximately two hours, including obtaining informed consent, information releases and self-report questionnaires. The computerized assessment recorded an average of 58 minutes (SD $\pm$ 23) of processing time per administration, which varied depending on the subject's complexity of condition and verbal output, and the interviewer's personal interaction style. The level of education for the interviewers ranged from some undergraduate college to M.D., and years of clinical experience ranged from 0 to 6 years post education.

A possible training effect was noted in which the earliest administrations took slightly longer than later interviews. A total of 11 interviewers administered the algorithm to 593 clinical subjects. The curve shows a moderate decrease in duration of assessment as interviewers gained experience over subsequent administrations; this was a non-significant

FIGURE 2. ASAM PPC1 Algorithm: Duration of Administration Learning Curve

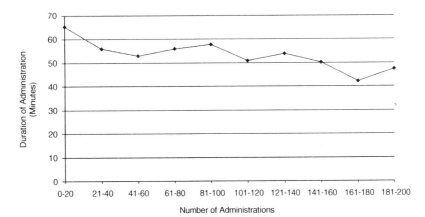

trend. There did not seem to be any clear relationship between educational level or years of clinical experience with duration of administration. The Level of Care placement decision (i.e., the blind assignment either matched or mismatched) was effectively displayed in real time, i.e., immediately upon completion of all data entry.

Ability to Distinguish Between Levels of Care

The findings are graphically depicted in Figures 3a-d, indicating that the ASAM Criteria appear to differentiate subjects according to several of the ASI Composite Scores and all of the RAATE subscales. Within the ASI, the strongest magnitude of differentiation was obtained on the Medical and Psychiatric Composite Scores. The three levels of severity are clearly delineated in a step-like fashion. The Drug, Legal and Family/Social Composite Score differences are not clinically as substantial and do not show the staircase pattern.

The RAATE differentiated subjects in the expected direction on all subscales and some of those differences were substantial in clinical magnitude. All of the RAATE subscales discriminated across groups in the expected staircase histogram pattern.

Expected differences were observed in the staircase histogram pattern for the symptom measures, including the CIWA, CINA and the 6-item Hamilton Depression Scale (Figure 3c). The Level IV group seemed to be differentiated in terms of being older and slightly less

FIGURE 3. Group Differences in Severity, Resistance, Symptom and Function Areas, by ASAM Level

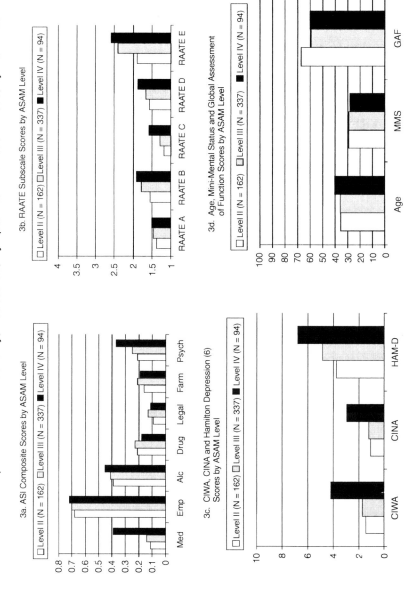

3a. ASI Composite Scores by ASAM Level

3b. RAATE Subscale Scores by ASAM Level

3c. CIWA, CINA and Hamilton Depression (6) Scores by ASAM Level

3d. Age, Mini-Mental Status and Global Assessment of Function Scores by ASAM Level

cognitively intact (Figure 3d). In terms of the GAF, both groups selected by the ASAM Criteria for inpatient care seemed to show poorer function than the group recommended for intensive outpatient care, i.e., Level II.

Table 3 displays the results of a multivariate ANOVA for the various instruments (F(34, 1148) = 9.65, p < .001). The item analysis reveals that several mean ASI composite scores significantly differentiate the

TABLE 3. For subjects determined by the ASAM Criteria to require three different levels of care, mean subscale scores across selected assessment instruments and significant differences.

Variable/Source	Level II (N = 162) Mean (SD)	Level III (N = 337) Mean (SD)	Level IV (N = 94) Mean (SD)	F(2,589)	F Prob.	Post-hoc t-tests
ASI Composite						
Medical	0.09 (.20)	0.15 (.24)	0.39 (.42)	40.15	0.001	II vs. IV III vs. IV
Employment	0.68 (.27)	0.70 (.28)	0.72 (.31)	0.60	0.550	N/A
Alcohol	0.39 (.32)	0.41 (.33)	0.45 (.34)	1.33	0.264	N/A
Drug	0.21 (.14)	0.23 (.14)	0.18 (.16)	4.17	0.016	III vs. IV
Legal	0.09 (.16)	0.13 (.20)	0.11 (.18)	3.91	0.021	II vs. III
Family	0.16 (.20)	0.21 (.22)	0.19 (.22)	2.38	0.093	N/A
Psychiatric	0.21 (.20)	0.25 (.22)	0.37 (.26)	15.10	0.001	II vs. IV III vs. IV
RAATE Subscale						
Resistance to Treatment	1.38 (.43)	1.47 (.42)	1.51 (.50)	3.53	0.030	II vs. IV
Resistance to Continuing Care	1.55 (.52)	1.78 (.52)	1.92 (.61)	16.69	0.001	II vs. IV
Biomedical Condition	1.18 (.30)	1.28 (.47)	1.58 (.64)	22.94	0.001	II vs. IV III vs. IV
Psychiatric Condition	1.57 (.39)	1.66 (.47)	1.87 (.64)	11.73	0.001	II vs. IV
Family & Environmental Obstacles	1.89 (.45)	2.40 (.58)	2.59 (.69)	59.09	0.001	II vs. III II vs. IV
CIWA Total	1.47 (2.14)	1.73 (2.18)	4.19 (4.13)	39.69	0.001	II vs. IV III vs. IV
CINA Total	1.04 (1.90)	1.21 (1.78)	2.95 (3.48)	27.56	0.001	II vs. IV III vs. IV
HAM-D	3.76 (2.58)	4.85 (3.22)	6.79 (3.73)	27.50	0.001	II vs. IV
Mini-Mental Status	29.18 (0.98)	29.01 (1.26)	28.04 (2.32)	21.31	0.001	II vs. IV III vs. IV
Global Assessment of Function	66.97 (11.59)	59.48 (14.39)	60.19 (13.39)	17.27	0.001	II vs. III II vs. IV

Levels of Care. Specifically, the Medical and Psychiatric composite scores show the strongest differentiation. The Employment and Family Composites failed to differentiate the groups. The Legal Composite Scores were significantly differentiated for Levels II vs. III. Also noteworthy is the fact that the Alcohol Composite Scores failed to differentiate the three Levels of Care, although the Drug Composite did, but not in the expected pattern.

With regard to the RAATE, the instrument's five subscales differentiated subjects in the expected directions with significance. Post-hoc tests of the subscales revealed clear differences, particularly between Levels II and Level IV. The distributions of scores is highly truncated, with most scales yielding scores near the floor of the potential distribution, possibly due to the volunteer, treatment-seeking nature of the study population.

Several additional measures were obtained on this sample. Both the CIWA, which measures alcohol withdrawal symptoms, and the CINA, which measures opiate withdrawal, demonstrated clear differentiation of Level IV from the other two levels. The six-item Hamilton Depression Index (HAM-D) differentiated Level II from Level IV as shown in Table 2. Results of the Mini-Mental Status examination also differentiated the groups. The lack of differentiation between Levels II and III is partially an artifact of the requirement that all study subjects (who had to qualify for either Level II or III) were to have evidence of clear cognitive function. This scale is also different from the others in that lower scores indicate greater dysfunction, and so Level IV patients were expected to have poorer MMS scores, as indeed they do. Finally, the Global Assessment of Function (GAF) scale (which does not contribute to the algorithm) shows a descending step function in which Levels III and IV have significantly worse function than the Level II group.

DISCUSSION

This work represents a comprehensive effort to fully implement and test a complex, hierarchical decision tree for substance abuse disorders treatment. Decision trees are gaining interest in the fields of addictions and mental health and some, such as these ASAM Criteria, are gaining widespread adoption. Over 20,000 organizations in the U.S. refer, treat, conduct research with, or pay for services for individuals with addictive disease. Currently many are mandated to use the ASAM Criteria to inform level of care. In the book form, the ASAM Criteria has sold over

10,000 copies. But as published, these criteria are not yet feasible standards, as the results of the present work with the ASAM Criteria make apparent. Results from the decision analysis raise serious concerns about whether clinicians can usefully apply the ASAM Criteria without computerization.

With the benefit of automation, data from these 593 administrations indicate that a rigorous adaptation can still yield a sufficiently concise interview for clinical purposes. The mean duration of administration, despite a wide range of instruments and assessment dimensions, was still less than one hour. Duration of administration may decrease along a gradual learning curve. A clinical version of an automated algorithm could easily eliminate unnecessary items within the three main feeder instruments (i.e., the ASI, the RAATE and the CIWA/CINA). These modifications would significantly reduce the administration time. Detailed analysis of the item pool from the current study will also indicate which items toward the Level of Care determination with the greatest weight, and which items are merely redundant. Streamlining the item pool in this way could also reduce the need for extensive training employed in this study to assure reliable administration of the original standard instruments (Baker et al., 2003). It may also be possible to re-structure the algorithm presentation sequence, e.g., so that some items can be skipped once it is clear that the patient is in need of immediate Level IV treatment.

Mapping of the ASAM Criteria decision rules to existing instruments is possible and is advantageous, permitting the process to be automated. The ASAM Criteria, when implemented in this fashion, appear to produce appropriate and, on many standardized subscales, significant differentiation between Levels (Figure 2a-d; Table 2). A differentiation in severity of bio-medical conditions is clearly evidenced for the three levels in the ASI Medical Composite and the RAATE Biomedical mean score. Severity of cognitive and psychiatric function across the three levels was apparent in the ASI Psychiatric Severity Composite, the RAATE Psychiatric Acuity mean, the Mini-Mental Status scores and the Global Assessment of Function scale scores. Differences across the Levels of Care were found in resistance to treatment as evidenced by the first two RAATE subscale scores. Social consequences and impediments to treatment success were evidenced weakly in the ASI Family Composite Score, but more strongly in the RAATE Family and Social Environmental Factors mean.

An interesting finding is the distribution of subjects classified by the algorithm into Level II (27.3%), Level III (52.8%), and Level IV

(15.9%). Since recruitment occurred at Level III detoxification centers for the majority of subjects, a preponderance of Level III assignments might be expected, whereas the 15.9% proportion gauged as needing Level IV might seem excessive. This interpretation is not clearly verifiable by the available data, however, as Massachusetts has relatively few Level IV detoxification programs for the indigent and Medicaid population under study. Therefore it is possible that the Level IV designation may be valid but due to unavailability, subjects were instead obligated to present to Level III programs. Whether disproportionate assignment reflects the need of the population or a bias in the ASAM Criteria can only be determined through outcome validity testing. Another limitation is that this study excluded subjects who could qualify for non-intensive outpatient care and therefore studies are needed to test the Level I characteristics of the ASAM Criteria.

These findings suggest that the hierarchical decision tree model that the authors of the ASAM Criteria sought to create may have succeeded in integrating diverse clinically relevant factors within the global Level of Care designations. The more important question for providers, managed care organizations and government, is whether matching according to these complex rules improves outcomes. The question of whether these rules have prognostic significance, much as cancer staging now offers, will await the differential outcomes of matching vs. mismatching. A prospective, controlled design, the ASAM Criteria Validity Study, is underway at this time.

REFERENCES

Allen, J., Kadden, R., 1995. Matching clients to alcohol treatments. Allyn & Bacon, Boston.

Alterman, A.I., O'Brien, C.P., McLellan, A.T., et al., 1994. Effectiveness and costs of inpatient versus day hospital cocaine rehabilitation. J Nerv Mental Dis 182, 157-163.

American Psychiatric Association, 1994. DSM-IV: Diagnostic and Statistical Manual of Mental Disorders, 4th ed. American Psychiatric Press, Washington, DC.

Baker S.L., Gastfriend D.R., 2003. Reliability of multidimensional substance abuse treatment matching: Implementing the ASAM Patient Placement Criteria. J Addict Dis 22(S), 45-60.

Bartlett, F.C., 1932. Remembering; a study in experimental and social psychology. The University Press, Cambridge.

Book, J., Harbim, H., Marques, C., et al., 1995. The ASAM's and Green Spring's alcohol and drug detoxification and rehabilitation criteria for utilization review. Am J Addiction 4(3), 187-197.

Brehmer, B., 1986. In one word: Not from experience. Cambridge University Press, Cambridge, England.

Center for Substance Abuse Treatment, 1995. The Role and Current Status of Patient Placement Criteria in the Treatment of Substance Use Disorders. Treatment Improvement Protocol (TIP) Series,13. Rockville, MD, Substance Abuse and Mental Health Services Administration. (SMA(95-3021)).

Chapman, L.J., Chapman, J.P., 1969. Illusory correlation as an obstacle to the use of valid psychodiagnostic signs. J Abnorm Psychol 74(3), 271-280.

Dawes, R., Corrigan, B., 1974. Linear models in decision making. Psychol Bull 81(2), 95-106.

Dawes, R.M., Faust, D., Meehl, P.E., 1989. Clinical versus Actuarial Judgment. Science 243, 1668-1674.

de Groot, A., 1965. Thought and choice in chess. Mouton, The Hague.

Fudala, P.J., Berkow, L.C., Fralich, J.L., et al., 1991. Use of naloxone in the assessment of opiate dependence. Life Sci 49(24), 1809-14.

Garb, H., 1989. Clinical Judgment, Clinical Training, and Professional Experience. Psychol Bull 105(3), 387-396.

Gastfriend, D.R., Filstead, W.J., Reif, S., et al., 1995. Validity of assessing treatment readiness in patients with substance use disorders. Am J Addictions 4(3), 254-260.

Gastfriend, D.R., McLellan, A.T., 1997. Treatment matching: Theoretic basis and practical implications. Med Clin North Am 81(4), 945-966.

Goldberg, L.R., 1969. The search for configural relationships in personality assessment: The diagnosis of psychosis vs. neurosis from the MMPI. Multivar Beh Res 4(4), 523-536.

Hamilton, M., 1960. A rating scale for depression. J Neurol Neurosur Psychiat 23, 56-62.

Hoffmann, N., Halikas, J., Mee-Lee, D., et al., 1991. American Society of Addiction Medicine–Patient Placement Criteria for the treatment of psychoactive substance use disorders. ASAM, Washington, DC.

Hogarth, R.M., 1987. Judgement and choice: The psychology of decision. Wiley, Chichester, England.

Holt, R.R., 1986. Clinical and statistical prediction: A retrospective and would-be integrative perspective. J Personality Assessment 50(3), 376-386.

Institute of Medicine, 1990a. Broadening the Base of Treatment for Alcohol Problems: A Report of a Study by a Committee of the Institute of Medicine, Division of Mental Health and Behavioral Medicine. National Academy Press, Washington, DC.

Institute of Medicine, 1990b. Treating Drug Problems. National Academy Press, Washington, DC.

Kahneman, D., Tversky, A., 1984. Choices, values, and frames. American Psychologist 39(4), 341-350.

Kleinmuntz, B., 1990. Why we still use our heads instead of formulas: Toward an integrative approach. Psychol Bull 107(3), 296-310.

Litt, M.D., Babor, T.F., DelBoca, F.K., et al., 1992. Types of alcoholics, II. Application of an empirically derived typology to treatment matching. Arch Gen Psychiatry 49(8), 609-614.

Longabaugh, R., Wirtz, P.W., DiClemente, C.C., et al., 1994. Issues in the development of client-treatment matching hypotheses. J Stud Alcohol Suppl. 12, 46-59.

Mattson, M.E., Allen, J.P., Longabaugh, R., et al., 1994. A chronological review of empirical studies matching alcoholic clients to treatment. J Stud Alcohol Suppl. 12, 16-29.

McKay, J.R., Cacciola, J.S., McLellan, A.T., et al., 1997. An initial evaluation of the psychosocial dimensions of the American Society of Addiction Medicine criteria for inpatient vs. intensive outpatient substance abuse rehabilitation. J Stud Alcohol 58:239-252.

McLellan, A., Kushner, H., Metzger, M., et al., 1992. The fifth edition of the Addiction Severity Index. J Subst Abuse Treat 9, 199-213.

McLellan, A.T., Luborsky, L., Woody, G.E., 1980. An improved diagnostic evaluation instrument for substance abuse patients: The Addiction Severity Index. J Nerv Ment Dis 168, 26-33.

Miller, G., 1956. The magical number 7, plus or minus 2–Some limits on our capacity for processing information. Psychol Rev 63, 81.

Miller, W., Brown, J., Simpson, T., et al., 1995. Chapter 2: What works? A methodological analysis of the alcohol treatment outcome literature. Handbook of Alcoholism Treatment Approaches. R. Hester and W. Miller. Needham, MA, Allyn and Bacon: 12-44.

Miller, W.R., Hester, R.K., 1989. Inpatient alcoholism treatment: Rules of evidence and burden of proof. American Psychologist 44(9), 1245-1246.

Morey, L., 1996. Patient placement criteria Linking typologies to managed care. Alc Health & Research World 20(1), 36-44.

Najavits, L.M., Gastfriend, D.R., Nakayama, E.Y., et al., 1997. A measure of readiness for substance abuse treatment: Psychometric properties of the RAATE research interview. Am J Addiction 6(1), 74-82.

O'Malley, S., Jaffe, A., Chang, G., et al., 1992. Naltrexone and coping skills therapy for alcohol dependence: A controlled study. Arch Gen Psychiatry 49(11), 881-887.

O'Sullivan, R., Fava, M., Agustin, C., et al., 1997. Sensitivity of the 6 item Hamilton Depression Rating Scale. Acta Psych Scandi 95(5), 379-384.

Payne, J.W., Bettman, J.R., 1992. Behavioral decision research: A constructive processing perspective. Annu Rev Psychol 43, 87-131.

Peachey, J., Lei, H., 1988. Assessment of opioid dependence with naloxone. Br J Addict 83(2), 193-201.

Pitz, G.F., Sachs, N.J., 1984. Judgment and decision: Theory and application. Ann Rev Psychol 35, 139-163.

Project MATCH Research Group, 1997. Matching alcoholism treatments to client heterogeneity: Project MATCH posttreatment drinking outcomes. J Stud Alcohol 58, 7-29.

Schwartz, S., Griffen, T., 1986. Medical thinking: The psychology of medical judgment and decision making. Spinger-Verlag, New York.

Sullivan, J.T., Sykora, K., Schneiderman, J., et al., 1989. Assessment of alcohol withdrawal: The revised Clinical Institute Withdrawal Assessment for Alcohol Scale. Br J Addict 84:1353-1357.

Teng, E., Chui, H., 1987. The modified "Mini-Mental State" examination. J Clin Psy 48, 314-318.

Tversky, A., Sattah, S., Slovic, P., 1988. Contingent weighting in judgment and choice. Psychol Rev 95(3), 371-384.

Congress, Office of Technology Assessment, 1983. The effectiveness and cost of alcoholism treatment. U.S. Government Printing Office, Washington, DC.

Volpicelli, J., Alterman, A., Hayashida, M., et al., 1992. Naltrexone in the treatment of alcohol dependence. Arch Gen Psychiatry 49(11), 876-880.

von Winterfeldt, D., Edwards, W., 1986. Decision analysis and behavioral research. Cambridge University Press, New York.

Predictive Validity
of the ASAM Patient Placement Criteria
for Naturalistically Matched
vs. Mismatched Alcoholism Patients

Stephen Magura, PhD, CSW
Graham Staines, PhD
Nicole Kosanke, PhD
Andrew Rosenblum, PhD
Jeffrey Foote, PhD
Alexander DeLuca, MD
Priti Bali, BA

Stephen Magura, Graham Staines, Nicole Kosanke, Andrew Rosenblum, and Priti Bali are affiliated with the Institute for Treatment and Services Research, National Development and Research Institutes (NDRI), New York, NY.

Jeffrey Foote was affiliated with the Smithers Treatment Center, St. Lukes-Roosevelt Medical Center, New York, NY at time of the study. Dr. Foote is currently affiliated with the National Center on Addiction and Substance Abuse, Columbia University, New York, NY.

Alexander DeLuca was affiliated with the Smithers Treatment Center, St. Lukes-Roosevelt Medical Center, New York, NY at time of the study. Dr. DeLuca is currently in private practice, New York, NY.

Address correspondence to: Dr. Stephen Magura, NDRI, 71 West 23rd Street, New York, NY 10010 (E-mail: magura@ndri.org).

David R. Gastfriend, MD and his staff at Massachusetts General Hospital provided valuable advice. Ann Geller, MD, significantly facilitated the initiation of the study. The assistance of the staff and patients at Smithers Treatment Center is greatly appreciated.

This study was supported by grant no. R01 AA10863 from the National Institute on Alcohol Abuse and Alcoholism, Bethesda, MD to Dr. Magura (Project Officer: Dr. Harold Perl).

An earlier version of this paper was presented at the American Society of Addiction Medicine (ASAM) 31st Annual Medical-Scientific Conference, Chicago, IL, April 15, 2000.

Reprinted with the permission from the *American Journal of Addiction* 2003; 12:386-397.

SUMMARY. This study examined the predictive validity of the ASAM Patient Placement Criteria for matching alcoholism patients to recommended levels of care. A cohort of 248 patients newly admitted to inpatient rehabilitation, intensive outpatient, or regular outpatient care was evaluated using both a computerized algorithm and a clinical evaluation protocol to determine whether they were naturalistically matched or mismatched to care. Outcomes were assessed 3 months after intake. One common type of undertreatment, i.e., receiving regular outpatient care when intensive outpatient care was recommended, predicted poorer drinking outcomes as compared with matched treatment, independent of actual level of care received. Overtreatment did not improve outcomes. There also was a trend for better outcomes with residential vs. intensive outpatient treatment, independent of matching. Results were robust for both methods of assessment. Corroboration by more research is needed, but the ASAM Criteria show promise for reducing both detrimental undertreatment and cost-inefficient overtreatment. *[Article copies available for a fee from The Haworth Document Delivery Service: 1-800-HAWORTH. E-mail address: <docdelivery@haworthpress.com> Website: <http://www. HaworthPress.com>]*

KEYWORDS. ASAM criteria, substance abuse treatment matching computer algorithm, predictive validity, treatment outcome

Standardized patient placement criteria (PPC) for objectively matching addiction patients an appropriate level of care (LOC) are not yet widely accepted among community programs, treatment funders and insurers.[1-6] PPC systems are underutilized because of doubts about their validity, concerns about their length and complexity, and conflicts among competing systems developed by treatment providers and managed care entities. A key question is: does prescriptive matching to levels of care make a difference in patient outcomes? Without well-validated placement criteria that justify intensive treatments on the basis of their greater effectiveness, the pressures of managed care to reduce costs will continue to threaten addiction treatment quality.[6-9]

The American Society of Addiction Medicine (ASAM) PPC are arguably the most prominent set of professionally-developed practice guidelines for matching addiction patients to suitable levels of care.[3,10] The ASAM PPC have strongly influenced other PPC systems and have led in the development of automated measurement technology to facilitate objective, replicable application of these criteria.

The research literature on the effectiveness of matching patients to levels of care is quite limited.[11] Although some studies have indicated that inpatient/residential and outpatient treatment have equivalent outcomes,[12,13] other research has found that patients with greater substance abuse severity, less social support, or psychiatric comorbidity benefit more from inpatient than outpatient treatment.[14,15] Alterman and colleagues[16] randomly assigned cocaine users who qualified for day hospital to either day hospital or inpatient treatment. Patients in both programs showed about equal improvement at a seven month follow-up, but day hospital costs were only 40% to 60% of inpatient costs; this study suggested that appropriate matching can be cost-effective.

The most detailed study completed to date indicated that, among cocaine addicts who met the original ASAM Criteria (PPC-1) for inpatient care, those receiving inpatient treatment (i.e., correctly matched to treatment) showed consistently better short-term (3 month) outcomes on a range of measures than did those receiving day hospital treatment (i.e., mismatched to a lower level of care).[17] The differential benefit for the correctly matched inpatients did not extend beyond three months, but no aftercare was received, which might explain this finding. The study also concluded that there were no other matching effects, but this seems attributable to an ambiguous hypothesis–that is, the study hypothesized that outcomes for mismatched patients should be poorer than for correctly matched patients. However, this does not take into account the directionality of potential mismatches. In particular, those patients meeting criteria for day hospital but receiving inpatient care should not be hypothesized to experience poorer outcomes than patients correctly matched to day hospital, but instead should be expected to experience equivalent outcomes. The reason is that presumed "overtreatment" should generally not be considered harmful, but rather constitutes an inefficient use of resources, which is a very different matter. Thus, McKay et al.'s finding[17] that these two cocaine user groups (i.e., correctly matched to day hospital vs. overtreated as inpatients) had equivalent outcomes actually supports the ASAM Criteria recommendation, in that cocaine users qualifying for day hospital should be assigned there, because a higher level of care (inpatient) does not provide increased benefit; this also was previously concluded by Alterman et al.[16]

Purpose of the Study. The current study examines the predictive validity of the ASAM PPC for matching alcoholism patients to different levels of care. The major hypotheses are:

1. Patients matched to the recommended level of care will have better outcomes than patients mismatched to a lower (less intensive) level of care, i.e., "undertreatment" is hypothesized to be detrimental.
2. Patients mismatched to a higher (more intensive) than recommended level of care will have outcomes no better than patients matched to the recommended level of care, i.e., "overtreatment" is neither beneficial nor detrimental (although it may be inefficient).

Recommendations for level of care were obtained for all patients using two alternative methods, a standardized computer-driven algorithm[18] and a clinical evaluation protocol. The matches and mismatches to level of care occurred "naturalistically" (as opposed to intentionally or experimentally), i.e., clinicians attempted to place patients in the clinically-recommended levels of care under "real world" conditions. When the attempt was successful, it is termed a "match," when unsuccessful, it is a "mismatch."

METHOD

Participants. Study subjects were alcohol dependent/abusing patients, as diagnosed by the Structured Clinical Interview for DSM-IV (SCID),[19] at Smithers Treatment Center, St. Lukes-Roosevelt Hospital, New York, NY. The sample included patients who were newly accepted for inpatient or outpatient treatment and also those who had been discharged from detoxification or residential care and were applying for continuing treatment. Applicants screened by Smithers medical staff and then referred for hospital detoxification (level IV) at other facilities were not included in the study; Smithers did not have level IV treatment available. The baseline study sample consists of 248 applicants who were interviewed and entered treatment during the 18-month period from April 1998 to September 1999.

Study Procedures. Smithers Treatment Center accepts patients who have an addiction problem, with public or private insurance coverage as well as self-pay. During the period of the study, Smithers offered treatment programs at three levels of care as defined by the ASAM PPC-1:[3] Regular Outpatient (Level I), with sessions of 1.5 hours on two evenings per week; Intensive Outpatient (Level II), which met 3.5 hours a day, five days a week; and Inpatient Rehabilitation (Level III), with a maximum stay of 28 days.

The study was located at the Smithers Evaluation Unit, where the study's baseline interviews were conducted as an extension of the regular intake assessment process. Eligible applicants were approached and invited to participate in the study in the sequential order of their appearance at the program on any day that interviewing occurred. The baseline interviews, which averaged 2.5 hours, contained the algorithm's "feeder" instruments (e.g., Addiction Severity Index [ASI]),[20] along with other standard scales. Follow-up interviews were conducted three months after study admission and consisted primarily of a subset of the baseline measures.

The current report focuses on one core outcome measure from the ASI follow-up: self-reported number of days in the past 30 days on which the patient consumed any alcohol. (This measure was also obtained at baseline.)

Level of Care (LOC) Matching. Recommendations for level of care were obtained for all patients using two alternative methods, a standardized computer-driven algorithm[18] and a clinical evaluation protocol. The algorithm's system for scoring the feeder instruments followed the ASAM PPC-1 guidelines for determining level of care recommendations. Accordingly, the algorithm generated scores on the six PPC-1 dimensions and an overall LOC recommendation. Clinicians also determined a level of care by conducting their own regular intake interviews, as well as having access to data collected through the algorithm feeder instruments. Clinicians rated each patient on each of the six PPC-1 dimensions and provided narrative explanations of their dimensional ratings.

Level of care matching was defined in terms of the congruence between the recommended LOC and the actual LOC received. Patients were classified as "matched" if the recommended and actual LOC were the same; as "undertreated" if the recommended level was higher than the actual level; and as "overtreated" if the recommended level was lower than the actual level. Undertreatment and overtreatment are termed "mismatches."

LOC matches/mismatches were determined separately for the algorithm and the clinician protocol, and separate outcome analyses were conducted for the algorithm and clinician determinations of LOC matches/mismatches. LOC matching and mismatching were not controlled by the treatment program or the researchers, but took place under naturalistic conditions. Clinicians were unaware of the algorithm's recommendations at intake; they attempted to implement the LOC recommendations produced by their clinician protocol, under the usual " real world" constraints.

In principle, the algorithm and the clinicians could recommend treatment at levels I, II, III, or IV. Because patients who needed hospital detoxification or other forms of hospitalization were excluded from the study by medical pre-screening, as indicated above, the clinicians' recommendations were limited in practice to levels I, II, or III. (Differences in LOC recommendations by the algorithm and clinician protocol are being examined in a separate paper.)

Logically, patients receiving level I treatment (regular outpatient) could not be overtreated according to either the algorithm or clinician protocol, since there is no "lower" level of treatment in the ASAM PPC-1; they would be defined as either matched to treatment (if the recommendation was level I) or undertreated (if the recommendation was level II, III, or IV). Patients receiving level II treatment (intensive outpatient) could be categorized as matched to treatment (if the recommendation was level II as well), undertreated (if the recommendation was level III or IV), or overtreated (if the recommendation was level I). Similarly, patients in level III (inpatient rehabilitation) could either be matched to treatment, undertreated or overtreated.

Adjustment to Algorithm Data for This Study. An adjustment to the algorithm-derived LOC recommendations was made for the purpose of the present analysis. Specifically, 17 applicants who were referred from inpatient detoxification facilities (level IV care) and recommended again for level IV by the algorithm were reclassified to a lower recommended level of care. Briefly, because of ambiguities in how certain medical and psychiatric assessment items were interpreted within the algorithm, the algorithm recommended 17 applicants in the baseline sample of 248 for detoxification at level IV, despite the fact that these applicants had recently been discharged from inpatient alcohol/drug detoxification at various local facilities. Virtually all these discharged patients had been abstinent for five days or longer and thus were not at withdrawal risk, nor did they have any acute medical or psychiatric problems that would have required immediate re-hospitalization.

It would not have been logical to define these patients as undertreated when entering treatment at an LOC of less than level IV, nor would this have been consistent with the intent of the ASAM PPC in our judgment. Consequently, we identified the specific assessment items that resulted in a level IV recommendation for these 17 applicants and determined a new algorithm-recommended level of care after these items were eliminated. Using this procedure, the originally recommended level IV care was reduced to level III for 11 applicants and to level II for 6 applicants; none was reduced to level I. The tables include this adjustment in algorithm-recommended levels of care.

Representativeness of Follow-Up Sample. Of the 248 patients in the baseline sample, 219 (88%) were located and interviewed at the 3 month follow-up. The reasons for the 29 cases of sample attrition were: subject location unknown (N = 26) and subject refusal (N = 3). Patients followed-up were more likely than those lost to follow-up to be age 35 or older (79% vs. 55%, p < .05) and to have had income above $200 in the month before admission (50% vs. 32%, p < .05). No significant differences were found on 10 other subject characteristics at intake.

RESULTS

Changes in Alcohol Use and Level of Care. Alcohol use declined substantially for the study cohort between intake and follow-up. The mean number of days of any alcohol use during the past 30 days declined significantly from 15.5 (s.d. = 9.5) at baseline to 4.5 (s.d. = 8.6) at follow-up (p < .001; paired t-test).

The 219 follow-up patients were classified into three categories based on the (initial) level of care they received at Smithers (regular outpatient [30%], intensive outpatient [18%], or inpatient rehabilitation [52%]) and compared on alcohol use at 3-month follow-up. The procedure was single-factor analysis of covariance where baseline drinking was the covariate and scores for drinking at follow-up (i.e., outcome measure) were log-transformed because of skewness.

There was a significant main effect for level of care (p < .001). Inspection of mean differences (untransformed scores) indicates that the higher the actual level of care received, the better were patients' alcohol use outcomes (i.e., fewer drinking days in past 30): regular outpatient care (mean = 7.2, N = 65), intensive outpatient care (mean = 4.8, N = 39), and inpatient rehabilitation (mean = 2.8, N = 115). In addition, the linearity of the effect of level of care on drinking was tested using multiple regression. With baseline alcohol use included as a predictor, there was a significant (linear) effect of level of care on (log-transformed) scores of alcohol use (p < .001).

Rates of Matching and Mismatching to Level of Care: As seen in Table 1a, the congruence between algorithm-recommended level of care and actual level of care received was 36% of patients matched, 44% undertreated, and 20% overtreated. The corresponding figures in Table

TABLE 1a. Actual Level of Care (LOC) by Algorithm-Recommended Level of Care

	Algorithm-Recommended LOC				Total
Actual LOC	I. Regular Outpatient	II. Intensive Outpatient	III. Inpatient Rehabilitation	IV. Hospitalization	
I. Regular Outpatient	**4 (2%)**	47 (21%)	8 (4%)	6 (3%)	65 (30%)
II. Intensive Outpatient	0 (0%)	**18 (8%)**	13 (6%)	8 (4%)	39 (18%)
III. Inpatient Rehabilitation	3 (1%)	41 (19%)	**56 (25%)**	15 (7%)	115 (52%)
Total	7 (3%)	106 (48%)	77 (35%)	29 (14%)	219 (100%)

Note. Bold cases are matched on LOC. Level IV recommendations were adjusted (see text).

TABLE 1b. Actual Level of Care (LOC) by Cliniican-Recommended Level of Care

	Clinician-Recommended LOC			Total
Actual LOC	I. Regular Outpatient	II. Intensive Outpatient	III. Inpatient Rehabilitation	
I. Regular Outpatient	**42 (19%)**	23 (11%)	0 (0%)	65 (30%)
II. Intensive Outpatient	1 (1%)	**35 (16%)**	3 (1%)	39 (18%)
III. Inpatient Rehabilitation	2 (1%)	32 (14%)	**81 (37%)**	115 (52%)
Total	45 (21%)	90 (41%)	84 (38%)	219 (100%)

Note. Bold cases are matched on LOC.

1b on congruence between clinician-recommended and actual level of care were 72% matched, 12% undertreated, and 16% overtreated. Subsequent measures of matching and mismatching to level of care that are employed in the analyses are based on these source data.

Matching to Level of Care and Outcomes. Three groups of patients–matched to LOC, undertreated, and overtreated–were compared on alcohol use at follow-up, separately for algorithm- and clinician-derived LOC recommendations. Again, based on single-factor analysis of covariance with baseline drinking as the covariate and log-transformed outcome scores, there were significant main effects for treatment matching/mismatching as defined by both the algorithm ($p < .01$) and clinician protocol ($p < .001$).

Mean differences (untransformed scores) indicate that undertreated patients exhibited poorer alcohol use outcomes as compared with either matched or overtreated patients, while the latter two groups had similar outcomes. For the algorithm, the means for days of alcohol use were:

overtreated (mean = 3.4, N = 44), matched (mean = 2.7, N = 78), and undertreated (mean = 6.4, N = 97). The corresponding means for days of alcohol use for the clinician protocol were: overtreated (mean = 1.7, N = 34), matched (mean = 4.1, N = 159), and undertreated (mean = 10.3, N = 26).

Multivariate Analyses–Algorithm Data. Multivariate analyses were undertaken to attempt to disentangle partial confounding between actual level of care received and matching/mismatching to level of care. The analyses also distinguished between specific types of undertreatment that characterized the sample in order to identify the location of effects. Multiple regressions on alcohol use at follow-up were conducted that included baseline alcohol use as a covariate and specific LOC matching and mismatching factors.

For algorithm-defined matching/mismatching, alcohol use at follow-up was regressed on the following predictors: (1) alcohol use at baseline, (2) level of care received (two indicator variables representing the three treatment levels–*Regular Outpatient* and *Intensive Outpatient*, with Inpatient Rehabilitation as the reference category), and (3) level of care matching/mismatching, as represented by these four indicator variables:

a. Outpatient treatment (I or II) recommended, but overtreated in Inpatient Rehabilitation (III);
b. Hospitalization (IV) recommended, but undertreated either in Inpatient Rehabilitation (III) or in Outpatient care (I or II);
c. Inpatient Rehabilitation (III) recommended, but undertreated in Outpatient care (I or II);
d. Intensive Outpatient care (II) recommended, but undertreated in Regular Outpatient care (I);

with "correct" match to level of care as the reference category.

Table 2a shows the direct effects of the predictor variables on alcohol use outcomes as represented by partial regression coefficients. More alcohol use days at follow-up were significantly predicted by more baseline alcohol days and being undertreated in Regular Outpatient care (i.e., receiving Regular Outpatient care whereas the algorithm recommended Intensive Outpatient care).

Days of alcohol use did not differ significantly between matched patients and those patients receiving *other* types of undertreatment or overtreatment as defined by the algorithm. There was a trend (p = .057)

TABLE 2a. Regressions of Alcohol Use at Follow-Up on Levels of Care and Matching/Mismatching as Defined by Algorithm (N = 219)

	Regression Coefficient	Stnd. Error	P-value
DV: Alcohol Days Past 30 (log)			
Baseline Alcohol Days	.03	.008	.000
Regular Outpatient (I) Received[a]	.03	.336	.940
Intensive Outpatient (II) Received[a]	.476	.249	.057
Outpatient (I) Recommended, but Overtreated in Rehab (III)[b]	.110	.222	.622
Hospitalization (IV) Recommended, but Undertreated in Rehab (III) or Outpatient (I, II)	.351	.252	.165
Inpatient Rehabilitation (III) Recommended, but Undertreated in Outpatient (I, II)[b]	.138	.327	.674
Intensive Outpatient (II) Recommended, but Undertreated in Reg Outpatient (I)[b]	.871	.365	.018

[a] Inpatient Rehabilitation is the reference category.
[b] "Matched to LOC" is the reference category.

for those receiving intensive outpatient treatment as opposed to inpatient rehabilitation to have more days of alcohol use at follow-up.

Multivariate Analyses–Clinician Assessment Data. For clinician-defined matching/mismatching, alcohol use at follow-up was regressed on the following predictors: (1) alcohol use at baseline, (2) level of care received (two indicator variables representing the three treatment levels–*Regular Outpatient* and *Intensive Outpatient*, with *Inpatient Rehabilitation* as the reference category), and (3) level of care matching/mismatching, as represented by two indicator variables:

a. Outpatient treatment (I or II) recommended, but overtreated in Inpatient Rehabilitation (III);
b. Intensive Outpatient care (II) or Inpatient Rehabilitation (III) recommended, but undertreated either in Regular Outpatient (I) or Intensive Outpatient care (II);

with "correct" match to level of care as the reference category.

More alcohol use days at follow-up were significantly predicted by more baseline alcohol days and being undertreated with the receipt of (mainly regular) outpatient care (Table 2b). Days of alcohol use did not differ significantly between matched patients and those receiving over-treatment as defined by the clinicians. There was a trend ($p = .075$) for those receiving Intensive Outpatient treatment as opposed to Inpatient Rehabilitation to show more alcohol use at follow-up.

Multivariate Analyses–Undertreatment Effects in Terms of Adjusted Means (Algorithm and Clinician Data). For both the algorithm- and clinician-derived data, the multivariate analyses also permit the significant undertreatment effect to be represented in terms of mean differences between groups. The mean scores on days of alcohol use (untransformed scores) were adjusted for level of care as well as alcohol use at admission. The two groups compared were: patients recommended for Intensive Outpatient care, but undertreated in Regular Outpatient care versus patients matched to Intensive Outpatient care.

For the algorithm-based data, the adjusted mean of days of alcohol use was higher for the undertreated patients (mean = 8.3, N = 47) than for those who were matched (mean = 2.7, N = 78). Similarly, for the clinician-based data, the adjusted mean was higher for the undertreated patients (mean = 9.2, N = 26) than for the matched (mean = 4.2, N = 159).

TABLE 2b. Regressions of Alcohol Use at Follow-Up on Levels of Care and Matching/Mismatching as Defined by Clinician (N = 219)

	Regression Coefficient	Stnd. Error	P-value
DV: Alcohol Days Past 30 (log)			
Baseline Alcohol Days	.024	.008	.004
Regular Outpatient (I) Received[a]	.349	.209	.097
Intensive Outpatient (II) Received[a]	.389	.218	.075
Outpatient (I) Recommended, but Overtreated in Rehab (III)[b,c]	−.289	.228	.206
Intensive Outpatient (II) or Rehab (III) Recommended, but Undertreated in Reg Outpatient (I)[b,d]	.538	.273	.050

[a] Inpatient Rehabilitation is the reference category.
[b] "Matched to LOC" is the reference category.
[c] Includes one patient recommended for regular outpatient, but overtreated in intensive outpatient.
[d] 88% of these patients were recommended for intensive outpatient but undertreated in regular outpatient.

DISCUSSION

The study's first hypothesis, that undertreatment would be associated with poorer treatment outcomes (i.e., more alcohol use at follow-up), was supported by the data based on both algorithm- and clinician-recommended levels of care. The size of the difference between undertreated and matched cases was similar for the two methods for assessing mismatching (i.e., approximately five days of alcohol use out of a possible 30). Similarly, the study's second hypothesis, that overtreatment and matched treatment would have similar outcomes, was supported by both the algorithm- and clinician-derived data.

Because actual level of care received and level of care matching were associated in these data, multivariate analysis was conducted to attempt to disentangle the two effects. This included distinguishing among several types of putative undertreatment that characterized the algorithm-derived data.

In the regressions for both the algorithm- and clinician-derived data, one specific type of undertreatment, receiving Regular Outpatient care although Intensive Outpatient care was recommended, predicted poorer alcohol use outcomes as compared with matched treatment; this effect was shown to be independent of the actual level of care received. The robustness of the result strongly indicates that applicants assessed as needing Intensive Outpatient treatment should receive such treatment, rather than the minimal group counseling that characterizes typical standard outpatient treatment. It also suggests that utilization of the ASAM PPC could help programs avoid certain types of detrimental undertreatment of alcoholism patients. Further, it underscores the risks of the behavioral health care system's pressures to reduce the intensity of substance abuse treatment without regard to validated placement criteria, and stresses the need for new strategies for overcoming patient resistance to clinical recommendations to enter more intensive treatment programs.

Again for both the algorithm- and clinician-derived data, the regression results indicated that, once statistical controls were introduced for LOC matching/mismatching effects (in addition to those for baseline alcohol use severity), patients receiving Inpatient Rehabilitation differed only marginally on alcohol use outcomes from patients receiving Intensive Outpatient treatment, and did not differ from those receiving Regular Outpatient care. Accordingly, these findings suggest that much of the apparent advantage of Inpatient Rehabilitation (Level III) over outpatient treatment (Levels I or II) in producing better outcomes is not independent of level of care matching effects. In other words, the prevalent view that alcohol use outcomes improve with treatment intensity requires the qualification that higher intensity may matter primarily insofar as it prevents detrimental undertreatment.

Two other types of undertreatment as *defined only by the algorithm* did not have statistically significant effects on alcohol use outcomes. (The pattern in the clinician-based data did not yield these two additional categories of presumptive undertreatment.) Patients recommended by the algorithm for hospitalization (Level IV), but mismatched to lower levels of treatment (Levels III, II, or I), did not fare significantly worse than patients matched to those lower levels of treatment. This suggests that the algorithm may have over-prescribed Level IV treatment in this sample. As noted previously, the program's medical staff did not recommend hospitalization for these applicants.

Similarly, patients recommended by the algorithm for Inpatient Rehabilitation (Level III), but mismatched to outpatient treatment (Level II), did not have poorer outcomes than patients matched to outpatient treatment. This suggests that the algorithm may also have over-prescribed Level III treatment. This conclusion must be tempered by the fact that the statistical power of the analysis is not high–there are only 21 undertreated patients of this type; a larger sample size might detect an undertreatment effect for this group.

We emphasize that these results are specific to the algorithm's interpretation of the ASAM Criteria. Comparisons with clinician-defined mismatching involving these additional categories of presumptive undertreatment are not available because the categories were almost non-existent in the clinician data. This is because clinicians were able to implement their own placement recommendations at a relatively high rate (72%) in this study, particularly their recommendations for Level III treatment which were readily accepted by Medicaid and some private insurers as well.[21] Thus, it is possible that additional categories of undertreatment, as more conservatively defined by the clinicians than by the algorithm, would show poorer outcomes in a setting which generates such additional categories.

In both the algorithm- and clinician-based data, patients presumptively overtreated by receiving Inpatient Rehabilitation and those matched to treatment had equivalent outcomes, after accounting for the effects of baseline alcohol use severity and actual level of care received. Although failure to find an effect can reflect insufficient statistical power as well as the absence of an effect in the population, the analyses reported did not show any appreciable nonsignificant trends. In short, overtreatment in Inpatient Rehabilitation confers no *additional* advantage to patients; but neither does such overtreatment appear to harm them.

Consequently, intentional overtreatment in Level III care does not seem to be justified on the basis of improved outcomes. The absence of a positive overtreatment effect supports cost-conscious limitation of substance abuse treatment to the recommended level of intensity. Efforts by managed care and others in behavioral health care delivery to reduce costs may be defensible, provided patients are assured of receiving the level of care recommended by validated placement criteria.

Study Limitations. It is difficult to guarantee certain proportions of matched and mismatched cases in a prospective study design, because extensive data must be collected, and actual placement must occur, before it can be determined whether a patient is matched or mismatched, as well as the specific type of mismatch.

Neither the algorithm- nor clinician-derived placement recommendations yielded coverage of the full range of possible categories of LOC matching and mismatching as defined by the ASAM PPC. Even among the categories that were populated by subjects, the patterns of partial coverage provided by each assessment method differed as well. Consequently, the study's hypotheses received only partial testing in this study.

Because matching and mismatching to level of care occurred "naturalistically," i.e., driven by situational constraints and circumstances, there is a possibility that one or more unmeasured factors could have produced a spurious relationship between LOC mismatching and alcohol use outcomes. However, the study was able to statistically control for two potentially important factors, patient baseline severity of alcohol use and actual level of care received. Note, however, that baseline severity is also a criterion for ASAM LOC recommendations, and thus controlling for this may actually lead to an *underestimate* of LOC mismatching effects.

The ASAM PPC were revised after the planning of this study and most recently published as the PPC-2R.[22] Although the revised criteria include additional sub-levels of care, the four primary levels (I, II, III, and IV) have remained, with essentially the same patient eligibility criteria. The computer algorithm is also being revised. Although it is likely that the main results of this study will be applicable to the revised criteria and algorithm, it is important that the revised criteria and algorithm undergo similar predictive validity testing in a variety of treatment settings and patients populations.

Summary. The data tend to support the study's original hypotheses, i.e., that matching to level of care is optimal, undertreatment is clinically harmful, and overtreatment is wasteful of resources. These preliminary conclusions, nevertheless, need to be corroborated by additional research if they are to attain general acceptance, especially in a changing behavioral health care system. In particular, the predictive validity of Level III (Inpatient Rehabilitation) matching recommendations in the ASAM PPC requires more investigation. Future research studies should employ multi-site designs that, by pooling data from heterogeneous samples, would provide greater statistical power and better distributions of matched and mismatched patients within each level of care.

Finally, the study indicates that the ASAM PPC as operationalized by a computer-driven algorithm shows considerable promise in rationalizing treatment recommendations for addiction patients. However, field research with the ASAM PPC should also aim towards reducing discrepancies in recommended levels of care generated by the computer algorithm vs. a clinician-driven assessment protocol.

REFERENCES

1. Hoffman NG, Halikas JA, Mee-Lee D. The Cleveland Admission, Discharge and Transfer Criteria: Model Chemical Dependency Treatment Programs. Cleveland, Northern Ohio Chemical Dependency Treatment Directors Association, 1987.

2. Weedman R. Admission continued stay and discharge criteria for adult alcoholism and drug dependence treatment services. Irvine, CA: National Association of Treatment Providers, 1987.

3. American Society of Addiction Medicine. Patient placement criteria for the treatment of psycho-active substance use disorders. Chevy Chase, MD: American Society of Addiction Medicine, 1991.

4. American Psychiatric Association. Work Group on Substance Use Disorders. Practice guidelines for the treatment of patients with substance use disorders: Alcohol, cocaine, opioids. American Journal of Psychiatry. 1995;152:11(suppl): 2-59.

5. Morey L. Patient placement criteria: Linking typologies to managed care. Alc Health & Rsh Wld. 1996; 20(1): 36-44.

6. Renz EA, Chung R, Fillman O, Mee-Lee D, Sayama M. The effect of managed care on the treatment outcome of substance use disorders. Gen Hosp Psych 1995; 17:287-292.

7. Fuller RF, Mattson ME, Allen JD et al. Multisite clinical trials in alcoholism treatment research: Organizational, methodological and management issues. J Stud Alcol, Suppl. 1994; 12: 30-37.

8. Book JD, Harbin HT, Marques CC, Silverman C, Lizanich-Aro S, Lazarus A. Should the ASAM criteria be adopted as a National Standard? In: A. Lazarus, ed. Con-

troversies in managed health care, Washington, DC: American Psychiatric Press, 1996: 143-158.

9. Mechanic D, Schlesinger M, McAlpine DD. Management of mental health and substance abuse services: State of the art and early results. The Milbank Quarterly. 1995; 73(1): 19-55.

10. American Society of Addiction Medicine. Patient placement criteria for the treatment of substance-related disorders. Second Edition. Chevy Chase: American Society of Addiction Medicine, Inc., 1996.

11. Gregoire TK. Factors associated with level of care assignment in substance abuse treatment. J Sub Abuse Treat. 2000; 18: 241-248.

12. Annis HM. Is inpatient rehabilitation of the alcoholic cost effective? A comparison. Advances in Alcoholism and Substance Abuse. 1986; 5: 175-190.

13. McKay JR, McLellan AT. An evaluation of the Cleveland criteria for inpatient treatment of substance abuse. Amer J Psychiatry. 1992;149: 1211-1218.

14. McLellan AT, Luborsky L, Woody GE, Druley KA, O'Brien CP. Predicting response to alcohol and drug abuse treatments: Role of psychiatric severity. Archives of General Psychiatry. 1983; 40: 620-625.

15. Miller WR, Hester RK. Inpatient alcoholism treatment: Who benefits? Amer Psych 1986; 41: 794-805.

16. Alterman AI, O'Brien CP, McLellan AT, August DS, Snider EC, Droba M, Cornish JW, Hall CP, Raphaelson AH, Schrade FX. Effectiveness and costs of inpatient versus day hospital cocaine rehabilitation. J Nerv & Mental Disease. 1994; 182 (3): 157-163.

17. McKay JR, Cacciola JS, McLellan T, Alterman A, Wirtz PW. An initial evaluation of the psychosocial dimensions of the American society of addiction medicine criteria for inpatient versus intensive outpatient substance abuse rehabilitation. J Stud Alc. 1997; 58: 239-252.

18. Turner WM, Turner KH, Reif S, Gutowski WE, Gastfriend DR. Feasibility of multidimensional substance abuse treatment matching: Automating the ASAM Patient Placement Criteria. Drug Alc Depend. 1999; 55: 35-43.

19. First M, Spitzer RL, Gibbon M, Williams JB. Structured clinical interview for DSM-IV Axis I Disorders (SCID-1). Washington, DC: American Psychiatric Press, 1997.

20. McLellan AT, Kushner H, Metzger D, Peters R, Smith I, Grissom G, Pettinati H, Argeriou M. The fifth edition of the Addiction Severity Index. J Sub Abuse Treat 1992; 9:19-21.

21. Kosanke N, Magura S, Staines G, Foote J, DeLuca A. Feasibility of matching alcohol patients to ASAM levels of care. Am J Addict 2002; 11:124-134.

22. Mee-Lee D, Shulman GD, Fishman M, Gastfriend DR, Griffith JH. ASAM patient placement criteria for the treatment of substance-related disorders, Second Edition-Revised. Chevy Chase, MD, American Society of Addiction Medicine, Inc., 2001.

Index

SPECIAL 25%-OFF DISCOUNT!

Order a copy of this book with this form or online at:
http://www.haworthpress.com/store/product.asp?sku=5144
Use Sale Code BOF25 in the online bookshop to receive 25% off!

Addiction Treatment Matching
Research Foundations of the American Society of Addiction Medicine (ASAM) *Criteria*

____ in softbound at $18.71 (regularly $24.95) (ISBN: 0-7890-2430-6)
____ in hardbound at $29.96 (regularly $39.95) (ISBN: 0-7890-2429-2)

COST OF BOOKS _____

Outside USA/ Canada/
Mexico: Add 20%. _____

POSTAGE & HANDLING _____

US: $4.00 for first book & $1.50
for each additional book
Outside US: $5.00 for first book
& $2.00 for each additional book.

SUBTOTAL _____

In Canada: add 7% GST. _____

STATE TAX _____

CA, IL, IN, MIN, NY, OH, & SD residents
please add appropriate local sales tax.

FINAL TOTAL _____

If paying in Canadian funds, convert
using the current exchange rate,
UNESCO coupons welcome.

❑ **BILL ME LATER:** ($5 service charge will be added)
Bill-me option is good on US/Canada/
Mexico orders only; not good to jobbers,
wholesalers, or subscription agencies.

❑ **Signature** _____

❑ **Payment Enclosed: $** _____

❑ **PLEASE CHARGE TO MY CREDIT CARD:**

❑ Visa ❑ MasterCard ❑ AmEx ❑ Discover
❑ Diner's Club ❑ Eurocard ❑ JCB

Account #_____

Exp Date _____

Signature _____
(Prices in US dollars and subject to change without notice.)

PLEASE PRINT ALL INFORMATION OR ATTACH YOUR BUSINESS CARD

Name

Address

City   State/Province   Zip/Postal Code

Country

Tel   Fax

E-Mail

May we use your e-mail address for confirmations and other types of information? ❑Yes❑ No
We appreciate receiving your e-mail address. Haworth would like to e-mail special discount
offers to you, as a preferred customer. **We will never share, rent, or exchange your e-mail
address.** We regard such actions as an invasion of your privacy.

Order From Your Local Bookstore or Directly From
The Haworth Press, Inc.
10 Alice Street, Binghamton, New York 13904-1580 • USA
Call Our toll-free number (1-800-429-6784) / Outside US/Canada: (607) 722-5857
Fax: 1-800-895-0582 / Outside US/Canada: (607) 771-0012
E-Mail your order to us: Orders@haworthpress.com

Please Photocopy this form for your personal use.
www.HaworthPress.com

BOF04